LIGHTING

THE

WORLD

LIGHTING
THE
WORLD

TRANSFORMING OUR ENERGY FUTURE BY
BRINGING ELECTRICITY TO EVERYONE

JIM ROGERS

WITH STEPHEN P. WILLIAMS

St. Martin's Press
New York

www.stmartins.com

Library of Congress Cataloging-in-Publication Data

Rogers, Jim E., 1947–
    Lighting the world : transforming our energy future by bringing electricity to everyone / Jim E. Rogers.
    pages   cm
        ISBN 978-1-137-27985-9 (hardback)—ISBN 978-1-4668-7936-2 (ebook)
    1. Rural electrification. 2. Energy industries. 3. Sustainable development.
I. Title.
    HD9688.A2R64   2015
    333.793'2—dc23
                                                                            2015007499

ISBN: 978-1-137-27985-9

Design by Letra Libre Inc.

First edition: August 2015

10 9 8 7 6 5 4 3 2 1

Dedicated to my grandchildren:

Alex, Emma, Will, Sara, Teddy,
Kate, Liza, and Maggie

CONTENTS

PROLOGUE

MY INTEREST IN THE LACK OF ACCESS TO ELECTRICITY began with a chance meeting in a remote Kenyan village. I came across a young man who was holding a cell phone in the middle of nowhere, with not a power line in sight.

"How do you charge that thing?" I asked.

"I walk three hours to the charging station," he said.

Wow, I thought. He walks six hours round-trip in one day to charge his cell phone. I can barely stand it when I check into a hotel and find there's not an outlet conveniently placed next to my bed.

A few months before this trip a friend had given my wife, MA, and me a small portable solar light made by a company called Little Sun. We used it often to walk our dog at night. I imagined what a difference a light like this could make in this young man's life.

Have you visited your doctor lately? Imagine if she'd had no choice but to examine you by candlelight, or worse, with no light at all. That's the scenario for one billion people around the world whose health clinics lack electricity.

Imagine attending third grade in a room entirely dependent on natural light. Or having to study at night by candlelight. Over half the primary school children in low-income countries learn like this, in rooms without power.

AS THE CEO of large US electrical utilities, I've spent most of my career providing electricity to millions of people. I'm talking about huge amounts of electricity, enough to power electric guitars, TVs, blenders, juicers, floodlights, lawn mowers, and can openers. Not to mention automobile factories, universities, hospitals, and other heavy power users. With all the power my companies have generated, I'm stunned by this fact: over one in six people worldwide lack access to electricity. That means 1.2 billion people[1] with no Internet. No water pumps. No bright lights to cook dinner by. Another billion or so have unreliable access.

There's no question that electricity is the foundation for economic development, education, health, and efficient farming. It is also a key driver in helping women gain equality at home, in the community, and at work.

Years ago I read *The Path to Power*, the first volume of Robert Caro's magnificent biography of President Lyndon Baines Johnson. One section described how the arrival of electricity in rural Texas transformed women's lives in a powerful way. This story helped define my mission as a young electricity utility CEO. I felt proud to be supplying power to millions of people, enabling them to live modern, healthier, and more productive lives. The book was another serendipitous signpost along my path to the present, where I hope to help solve the problem of energy access for the 1.2 billion people on earth who lack electricity.

It's our obligation to assist people who lack power in their quest to get ahead and take better care of their families. It is a human imperative.

A lot of powerful and influential people talk often about income equality and equal rights for women. But hardly any of them talk about electricity. This is a huge blind spot. For example, if you investigate development issues in Africa, you'll read about the lack of clean cook stoves, vaccines, education, and health care, a lack that profoundly affects women and families. But you won't read much at all about the fact that electricity is the foundation for all of these basic human needs. Once people have electrical power, suddenly they are able to address many other seemingly intractable inequities.

There are fine minds working on this dilemma, all around the world. But most are working in isolation, on a small scale. I'd like to go large. I believe that together, we can make access to electricity a basic human right. And then we can work together globally to make that right a reality.

I've approached the issue as a very curious student with a relatively solid background in the interplay of the provision of electricity and government regulation. No one has yet cracked the code on how to create scalable, affordable, and sustainable access to cost-effective power. I haven't found the magic bullet either, but I believe that, when we synthesize all the disparate innovations on the horizon right now, we will be well on our way. I've come to realize that, of all the factors limiting access to electricity, sustainability is the most important. That factor includes financing, technology, ownership, the environment, and a host of other issues.

Most of the efforts to bring power to those without it in the last 20 years have involved a mix of philanthropic and profitable ventures. There's a pretty broad consensus now, among the many people who have been working in this arena, that for-profit approaches have better long-term results. People need to pay for their power, and profit from it too with higher standards of living.

Ownership. Respect. Engagement. Desire. Ambition. Acceptance of cultural differences. All these factors play key roles in how rural villagers enable themselves to install power in their homes and businesses. For too long, Western financing and other commitments have gone to leaders of low-income countries with "sophisticated" or "better"—that is, more "Western"—ideas about how to improve the lives of their people. I propose that we instead try to learn from the people themselves. Villages and countries have unique characteristics that must be understood and respected by anyone who is coming in from the outside to offer advice or set up a business. In fact, the efforts of these villagers with clean energy might, in the long run, teach us how to rescue our own deteriorating infrastructure.

Of course, I wouldn't be working on this issue at all if I didn't believe that people like me, who've worked for large utilities in the high-income world, also have a lot to offer to places that lack access to electricity. I think we have the opportunity right now to help about 600 million people in a few dozen countries in Sub-Saharan Africa, about 300 million people in India, about 300 million in the rest of Asia, and millions more in Latin America and the Middle East who now live in the dark.[2] That's not to mention the other one billion people in the world who might have a link to a grid, but still don't have a reliable, 24/7 supply because that grid is not so good.

We do have precedent for such a project. In the 1930s and '40s, the United States electrified almost all the rural areas of the country (save for a few glaring, and inexcusable oversights, such as the Navajo lands, where tens of thousands of the descendants of America's original inhabitants still lack access to electricity). We did this by offering government-guaranteed, low-cost money to rural electric co-ops.

We'll have to do a similar thing around the world in order to bring electricity to the 1.2. Ideally, governments in the low-income world would create franchises in the rural areas with the appropriate rules and regulations. With these franchises in place, the private company that wins the right to serve an area would be able to attract the capital necessary to bring electricity to the people there.

What is missing today is the political will to create these franchise areas alongside the state-owned utilities. As of now, the state-owned enterprises don't have the capital to expand into rural areas. These franchises will let private business raise those funds. There's enough money available in government aid programs, investment capital, and development finance to address the issue. What are missing are the intent and the political will to create these franchises side by side with the state-owned utilities.

I think we can create political will by making access to power a basic human right that is recognized as such by the United Nations and governments around the world. And why would anyone deny that electricity is a right? Electricity is the backbone of health care, education, clean water, hygiene, food safety, and many other vital human interests. And now that we're inescapably in the digital age, everyone needs electricity for access to the Internet and telephones and TV. I cannot accept that we would deny more than one in six people on earth access to the most basic and revolutionary change in our culture in the last century. A first step toward making electricity a basic human right will be for the UN to include it as one of its sustainable development goals.

We can't bring electricity to the rural areas of the world using an old-fashioned industrial grid based on building more coal plants and running copper lines from timber pole to timber pole across Sub-Saharan Africa, or by running cables underwater to connect the archipelago of Indonesia. The environment and financial impediments make that impossible. Instead, we'll do it with modern technology: solar and other clean energy sources, new kinds of batteries, LED lights, efficient cook stoves and TVs, and plenty of innovations that are now surfacing. We believe that with the drop in solar panel prices in the last decade, solar is a much cheaper alternative to grid power for people in rural areas. We don't know what the future holds, but I'm certain new technologies will appear to surprise and delight us all.

Let me tell you, we're going to change the world for the better. Access to electricity is becoming more crucial as the Internet transforms education, banking, employment, and political thinking. The Internet allows people to participate in the global culture and in economic exchange. It's become widely accepted that access to the Internet should be a basic human right in the twenty-first century. In a sense, it allows people to be free. Electricity is essential to becoming an informed and effective member of society. Everyone should have that chance.

With universal access to electricity there is a good chance that in some rural town a twenty-first century Edison will team up with a twenty-first century Steve Jobs to create a new energy source that will lead us all safely into the future.

MY FIRST STAB at the access challenge was to cofound the Global BrightLight Foundation, which has distributed more than 60,000 combination solar lanterns and cell phone chargers in Rwanda, Uganda, Zambia, Nepal, Peru, Bolivia, Haiti, and Guatemala. After starting with a philanthropic approach, we quickly shifted to a market model, in which we recycled the proceeds from sales to buy and distribute more solar lanterns.

Soon after, as the chair of the Global Sustainable Electricity Partnership (GSEP), a consortium of 13 of the world's largest electric utilities, I led Duke Energy and several other companies in GSEP in an effort to bring sustainable electricity to Cochico, a remote village in Patagonia, Argentina. Together, we built a microhydro facility that gave a regional primary school access to electricity almost 24 hours a day rather than the only four hours a day supplied by a diesel generator. These are important steps, but small efforts compared to what is to come.

Right now there are about the same number of people on earth living without electricity as there were when Edison lit his first lightbulb. Before 1882, when Edison's Pearl Street power plant came to life in New York, people with money burned oil to light their homes. First it was whale oil. That slowly gave way to kerosene, the fuel that built the first Rockefeller fortune. Amazingly, 134 years later, hundreds of millions are still burning kerosene.

Please don't misunderstand. I know that providing access to power is an enormous challenge and great strides have already been taken, as I will discuss in this book. Despite all the innovative ideas and efforts from NGOs, foundations, businesses, and governments, a model is still needed that can overcome the barriers to scaling up. These roadblocks include government interference, technology hurdles, finance gaps, the limited financial resources of the rural poor, and the lack of local understanding of the routine operation and maintenance of facilities.

But I'm increasingly convinced we can solve these issues. We have proven we can do this in the high-income world, where we are able to deliver electricity in a way that balances affordability with reliability, sustainability, and increasingly clean production. By drawing on our own experiences, we may bring real light to the remotest areas of the world in a way that sustains us all.

I've written this book in order to shine a spotlight on the challenge of helping the 1.2 have access to the electricity they deserve. I offer my view of the way forward as one option. I hope this inspires other thinkers and doers to join the cause and make this access a priority for governments, businesses, foundations, and villagers all over the world.

1

A VISION OF
WHAT WILL BE

WHILE THERE IS AS YET NO SUCH PLACE, I KNOW THAT, about 15 years from now, I will live in this world:

As I leave my well-lit home in Charlotte, North Carolina, the lights go off and the air-conditioning stills, all automatically. We've finally started to take energy use seriously in America, and I'm pleased. As I drive across the leafy city to the airport, off-grid streetlights flicker on, their nighttime power guaranteed by small, durable batteries. I board my flight and travel through the night and most of the day until I'm over East Africa at dusk.

I could swear it's brighter now than it used to be, even from thousands of feet in the air, but that can't be right. More villages are lit up, but less light is wasted. It's rare these days to see bright cities at night, especially in the US. The brightness on the ground, in thousands of villages and urban neighborhoods, is more subtle than it was in the first quarter of the century, when cities still lit themselves like torches, and people expected streets to be bright as day, even after midnight.

It's not just lights that are being conserved. I remember people leaving their houses clutching sweaters on 95-degree days because they knew the air in the shopping mall would be too cold. Given all that was happening with climate change, it became clear that we had to do things differently. And as a global culture we did just that, and faster than I would have ever thought possible.

But the beautiful part is that we still aren't deprived. We haven't given up light. We haven't given up computers. We haven't given up air-conditioning. Instead, we've learned, and are still learning, how to generate power in a less harmful way, and also how to use it more efficiently—only when we need it, rather than 24/7.

After 14 hours, the pilot announces that we are preparing to land in Kigali, Rwanda. Now here is a place that has changed dramatically. In 2015, less than 10 percent of the people in the country had steady access to electricity, but now the countryside is twinkling with lights. The country has done an amazing job of building out its grid, now powered by gas from methane ice crystals harvested from the depths of Lake Kivu, and by solar power, wind, and hydro power. At the same time, it has built up a market for efficient TVs and lights and other devices. Since the country now has a decent power supply for the first time in its history, it is even starting to create local entrepreneurs who are supplying parts to the larger appliance manufacturers, printing much of their inventory on 3-D printers. Everyone assumes that within the decade they'll be manufacturing the actual appliances here, because those big companies are looking at the Kigali area as a place not only to do business, but also to make their products. Rwanda has always had smart people and plenty of desire, but until recently it didn't have reliable, affordable electrical power and all the services that come with it.

The hills, once the scene of horrific genocide, are now packed with wind turbines spinning to feed the many large microgrids that dot the city, generating electricity for the main grid as well as backing it up when it fails. As the plane descends, I notice that many rooftops are covered with large solar panels, some to feed factories and stores, others supplying electricity to private homes and the grid. It's thrilling to see so much power in the works.

THE ELECTRIC TRAM from the airport is swift and comfortable, crowded though it is with men in suits, some women in Western attire, and others in traditional Rwandan patterns and head wraps. The tram stops at stations in some very poor areas of the capital to pick up and let off passengers. It stops at the Gisozi Memorial Genocide Centre, which, from what I can see, appears to be powered by a solar-wind hybrid microgrid.

This country, which once violated the most basic human right of over 800,000 people, was among the first to embrace the UN initiative to make access to electricity a basic human right, on par with life, food, health care, and water. It was a remarkable transition for the country, and a great boost for the UN's mission.

I'd long thought that getting the UN to recognize the vital importance of electricity as the foundation of all the other human rights was essential. Many people worked long and hard to get that resolution passed, and when it happened, I watched as country after country embraced the concept. That in turn prompted their governments to focus on increasing access to electricity. Tariffs on solar equipment were reduced. International money flowed more easily into countries that were prioritizing electricity and abandoning economic and legal barriers to getting it. It was a remarkable effort.

I awake early and eat breakfast on the terrace overlooking the city. Below, a fleet of electric vehicles are charging at a solar microgrid. I can see their sleek shapes in the gaps between the solar panels, which are slanted at this hour to capture the maximum yield of the strong morning sun. Japanese auto makers were quick to spot the market for all-terrain electric vehicles with long-life batteries— vehicles capable of taking people into the distant reaches of countries like Rwanda—but American, Chinese, and Indian manufacturers soon caught up. Now, there's a huge market for durable electric vehicles in what were once called the developing countries. These days they should be called re-innovating countries.

If anything, they've surpassed us. These countries are consistently on the cutting edge of energy, communication, and innovation. I hope that we in the West will catch up soon, although we have the larger hurdle of dismantling our previous industrial grid and manufacturing system and replacing it with something more like that of Rwanda. The world has truly shifted, and wise companies are spotting opportunity. Those whose interests are entrenched in the old ideas will quickly fall by the wayside.

After I've had some yogurt and fruit, Ali, a representative of the village of Nyabarongo, comes to collect me so I can get out and see these astonishing changes up close.

"WE'RE DOING GREAT!" he says when I ask about life in his village. "You'll see. It hasn't been as much about new technology as it's been about new ideas we had about how to move forward. We got a lot of help from outside experts—and from studying on our own.

But in the end, it came down to us wanting something different, and making it happen."

We drive in one of the electric vehicles through busy intersections marked by sophisticated stoplights that not only tell cars to stop or go, but also warn the numerous pedestrians about oncoming traffic. The activity at these intersections is relayed wirelessly to a central station that keeps the traffic flowing smoothly—the entire traffic flow system is powered by various microgrids that can be called on to join forces when more power is needed.

Soon we leave the city behind. Set back from the side of the road here and there are brick homes in which families live primarily on what they can grow. They eat most of the squash and potatoes, bananas and beans from small plots themselves, and sell any crops that are left over. This is how rural Rwandans have lived for centuries, and it works, in many ways. But today's subsistence farmers have a distinct advantage over their ancestors: power, generated by the sun and stored in batteries, to run water pumps, radios, lights, and even refrigerators and cook stoves.

We take a left off the main road, heading deeper into the countryside. The pavement soon turns to red earth. On either side of us vacant hills spread nearly empty except for grazing cattle. All the trees were cut down years before for fuel. I wonder how people feel about having decimated so much forestland, now that they have efficient electric cooktops and solar ovens that work just as well as gas or wood-burning models. I'm sure they wish this progress had come sooner, so they were still surrounded by shade trees and songbirds.

Soon we come to a village of perhaps 50 well-cared-for brick homes, surrounding a broad, shady dirt plaza. There's a church at one end and a small store at the other. Solar streetlights stand tall in front of each. We stop for a bottle of water, and I notice electrical lines running from a small building to the church. On top of the building are a few solar panels. The woman who runs the store tells me that the church got solar power several years before. Kids from the village study there at night for free, she says. However, many of the houses here are still without electricity, which is puzzling, given all the possible ways people could obtain light. She says the residents of the community have a lot of trouble working together, and they have not been able to figure out how to build and manage a good microgrid. Some of them have solar home systems, but most don't share. The interior of her own store is lit by three very bright LED hanging lamps.

"One of these days we're going to figure it out," she says, laughing.

Ali and I drive on for about ten miles into the countryside until the distant landscape starts to look surprisingly green. Unnaturally green, I think.

"What's going on?" I ask Ali.

"It's the solar irrigation pumps," he says. "It's a small miracle, really. We printed them from plans we got online."

Outside his village is one of the most ambitious off-grid irrigation projects I've ever seen. It's a community effort, in which each villager is able to apply for a parcel of land to work. Amazingly, where once there was dry, washed-out earth, now there is a fertile farm divided into individual plots.

In the past, some families grew maize and other foods in the land around their houses, and women carried water jugs on their heads from the central village pump to water the plants. It was hard, inefficient work, and the results were rarely great. And in addition to carrying water for their gardens, the women had to carry more water home for their families, who had little to eat. Many suffered from malnutrition.

These days, 40 or 50 village families work the small plots and produce a surprising amount of food. These solar-irrigated gardens can yield several thousand pounds of food per harvest. A lot of that goes to feed the families, or is sold cheaply to the other villagers, but at least a third of it is sent to other parts of the country. The community has organized a truck for delivering goods to market, and they have tools that everyone pays for on a rental basis. They grow as much as they can, and sell any excess to people as far away as Kigali. The new electric buses, run by the government, make getting around a lot easier than it used to be.

The result of this solar irrigation: families boost their incomes while cutting food costs and improving their diets.

Ali explains to me that financing and installing the 3-D printed solar irrigation pumps was not easy. The villagers couldn't come up with the thousands of dollars that were needed to get the system running. But, working with an organization in Kigali, they were able to finance the purchase. Several villagers were trained to manage and service the pumps. Then, after a long wait for the equipment to be printed, they started the farm. Now the families who cultivate crops dedicate a small percentage of their market earnings to a cooperative fund that repays the original loan and maintains enough money to cover the cost of repairs, pay the people who service the pumps, and contribute to a savings account to pay for more equipment so more families can participate. Their goal, over the next five years, is to have a plot of irrigated land for every family in the village that wants one.

We park the car at a battery charging station at the edge of the village, a few hundred yards past the boundary of the farm. I'm completely amazed by this, because we're in the middle of nowhere. I don't think even Elon Musk saw this coming when he invented the Tesla. Our driver buys a prepaid charging card. He plugs the car in, types the card's code into the charger. Ali and I go off to wander the village while our vehicle is topped off. Our driver stays with the car, of course. It's his baby.

The main street of this village is crackling with life, with lots of people on foot, and young and old alike gliding past on bicycles and motorbikes. The road is lined with brick storefronts that open to the street with goods piled in front under the overhanging roofs. There is a bed store with mattresses on display in front, a hardware store, and a phone and mobile banking kiosk. A couple of little groceries sell candles and scarves, headphones, and LED lightbulbs in addition to more usual fare. In the old days, there would be racks of phones that people had left for charging, but now, it seems, that business model has been phased out. A 3-D print shop powered by a powerful solar-wind hybrid makes useful objects and parts next door.

Nyabarongo was founded 30 years earlier by Congolese refugees fleeing "the armed men" who made life impossible. The refugees were given land here, and some metal for their roofs. They dug clay and dirt and cooked their own bricks to make the village houses. They dug wells and built up small businesses out of thin air, but life was still difficult, and it seemed there was little hope of relief, let alone prosperity. And then one of the village families managed to buy a simple LED lamp that could be charged with a little solar panel. That lamp allowed the kids to study, and let the mother earn a little extra money in the evenings by weaving baskets in the traditional style. Soon, the father invested in a more powerful solar system that allowed him to charge phones, for a fee. Within a year, it became clear to the rest of the village that the sun allowed this family to raise their standard of living by an extraordinary measure, and others got interested.

All of this interest fit well with the Rwandan government's plans to bring electricity to the entire country, and the village's obvious self-motivation drew the attention of a few agencies that were directing equipment and expertise to the countryside. A for-profit company founded in the United States had picked Rwanda as its first market in which to introduce solar home systems and microgrids, in a partnership with the Rwandan government. The residents formed a committee and named several people to study to become solar engineers. They installed simple lighting and charging systems in many homes in the village.

As the years went by, the US company's local representatives convinced the villagers to invest in a hybrid microgrid, based on wind and solar. The costs were very high and the villagers weren't sure they could afford it, even though they'd seen the standard of living rise across the board in the village.

In the end, the villagers and their Rwandan partners formed a local utility that purchased, installed, and maintained the equipment. Payment is made via mobile phone. All the data about usage, demand, generation, and distribution is gathered into computers and processed with algorithms designed to keep everything running efficiently. I'm pleased to see that the microgrid is working, that it is sustainable, and that it is supported and funded by villagers. They have a large stake in its success, and its success is due to their interest.

As we walk through the village I am struck by how neat and tidy most of the homes are, with living fences made of thorny green plants surrounding most front yards, and flowers planted around the entry porches. Some of the homes still have solar panels on their roofs, reminders of the original home solar systems, and, in truth, a good backup in case the three microgrids, each powering 75 families, fail.

A woman named Uwimana and her husband, Théophile, invite us into their home where they are raising three kids. A streaming radio tuned to the local community station advertises goods to swap—a chair for a pitcher, someone has a cow for sale—the kinds of things I remember from the radio swap meet when I was growing up in Kentucky. And then I hear someone offering to swap a digital game player for a solar flashlight, and I realize that times have changed.

The interior of the home is mostly lit by daylight, but LED bulbs light any areas that need it. An iron kettle of beans simmers on an induction range in the kitchen, and I can smell something baking in the oven. The husband explains to me that this range has the highest efficiency rating of any on the market.

"I'm paying for it with the cassava bread I sell," says Uwimana. Her husband smiles broadly.

They also have a large low-energy flat-screen television on the wall. A tablet computer sits on the table. They use it to research whatever they want. Health information. Exchange rates. The best natural pesticides for keeping beetles away from pumpkin vines. And, of course, music videos and movies. The entire village has wireless Internet access as part of a Rwandan government initiative meant to encourage villagers to figure out how to get electricity for themselves. It turned out that Internet access, along with the thought of being able to watch soccer games and dramas on TV, was one of the biggest motivators for getting people to invest in high-powered microgrids. (Whatever reason drives people to buy energy-efficient appliances is OK with me, because, as the saying goes, the cleanest and cheapest energy is that which you do not use.)

On the way back to the car I notice a line in front of a larger brick building at the edge of a soccer field, so we walk over there. This turns out to be the health clinic for the area, run by a cooperative system supported by the government and several outside agencies. Families can buy insurance and get affordable treatment for most illnesses here.

Ali and I decide to go inside, and approach the fully digital front desk. The head nurse gives us a tour of some treatment rooms with modern equipment. The clinic has its own microgrid, including a dedicated solar system with a good battery for nighttime energy storage. The system even allows the nurses to perform X-rays and diagnostic tests that require a lot of power. And each piece of equipment is networked, able to communicate its status and energy needs to the microgrid as part of what we used to call the Internet of Things, but now just think of as part of everyday life.

Leaving the village, car battery fully charged by the sun, we head back toward Kigali. As we pass through other villages that haven't achieved quite the success of Nyabarongo, I realize that Nyabarongo has leaped across a century in the last 15 years, skipping the entire age of Edison and the industrial grid system that first made America powerful so long ago. This village is a vision of a clean future, and reflects the age of enlightenment that many African nations, India, and other countries are bringing to the world at large. It's a future that can be real, if we decide to listen.

2

DARKNESS VISIBLE

A FRIEND OF MINE ONCE CHOSE TO MOVE WITH HIS wife to an Andean cloud forest cabin that had no electricity or running water, except for a pump out in the yard. The couple, writers from Manhattan, had romantic ideas about what it would be like to live as people did before the age of Edison, and they wanted to start a family. They'd work on books during the day—a novel for him, poetry for her—and work on making a baby after the sun went down. Life at its purest, or so they thought, under star-filled skies unmarred by light pollution.

Purity means different things to different people. Not surprisingly, the locals who lived in the area saw the situation differently. They knew all about the usefulness of electricity from their trips up the mountains to visit the nearest market town. People could read at night there. Doctors had refrigerators for vaccines. People could make a pitcher of passion fruit juice in an electric blender with no trouble at all.

My writer friend had always taken this type of convenience for granted: he would soon learn how lucky he'd been.

To get to their new home they hired a truck to take them on a dirt road over an extinct volcano called Cotacachi and into a zone in which some people had power and others didn't. At the village of Santa Rosa, a small track led down past the primary school, into the countryside. Santa Rosa had received electricity about a year before, and now, with streetlights and porch lights shining, the pueblo was a lot livelier at night. The schoolyard was now a gathering point for the community, with soccer games and festivals. My friend and his wife left the bus there and set out on foot down the trail toward their new home.

The first farmhouse they passed was dark. The family living on this farm, called El Refugio, cooked with a propane stove, and used candles and kerosene to light their evenings, when necessary. Without a refrigerator, the single mother had no way to store milk for her four young children. Though the kids all attended the school just up the road, they weren't able to study at night unless they walked up to the village and sat with their neighbors.

Farther along the trail, past a field of sugarcane and below a mountain covered in old-growth cloud forest, were the lightless cinderblock homes of subsistence farmers. Nearby was the grand house of an old hacienda, but it too lacked electricity and the outhouse door hung open in the rear garden.

As my friends continued into the forest, they came to a rustic log bridge over a fast stream. To the left was a 30-foot high waterfall. This section of the trail, deep beneath the thick canopy of trees, was dark as ink at night, without even a view of the stars. A hundred yards farther brought them to the small homestead called El Placer ("the pleasure"), an old, three-room wooden farmhouse. It had murals of volcanoes painted on its walls, and a long, beautiful view across a valley to the distant mountains, but no electricity.

In this house near the equator, dusk descended at 6:00 p.m., and darkness fell like a hammer soon after—there was none of the lingering twilight so beloved by the northern European poets my friends had romanticized. The loss of light at this latitude, in which most of the world's poor and powerless live, is sudden and brutal, a daily reminder of what is missing. For eleven and a half hours the only light came from the stars and the moon, and whatever man-made devices a person could pull together—kerosene lamp, candle, or perhaps a flashlight, although replacement batteries were at least an hour's walk away. With such a long night, there wasn't much time for chores like cooking and cleaning, which had to be taken care of by late afternoon.

There was no radio, no TV, and no news, football scores, or music. The couple couldn't charge a cell phone, and anyway, with no cell towers nearby, there was no reception. To find a signal they had to climb the ridge to a little store that had good reception, and also charged phones, for a fee. This was where people came to use mobile payment to send money to their kids away at school (there was no high school in the valley), or to see if the distributor had put money in their account in payment for that load of lemons they had harvested and carried up to the road last week.

In this valley, when a kid woke up in the middle of the night with a fever, there was no way to see clearly what her eyes looked like—were they rheumy? Was there discharge? Maybe her forehead felt hot, but, without sufficient light, it was hard to make out the reading on the thermometer. The toilet out back, an outhouse, was lit by a candle. What if it set the whole thing on fire?

A neighbor about half a mile up the mountain lost her whole house when an oil lamp—a small, one-pint can of kerosene with a wick sticking out of the top—tipped over, spreading flame across the table and the floor and igniting the plank walls. Luckily, no one was killed, but the woman burned her hand terribly trying to get her son to safety. She had to sit through the dark night in awful pain, waiting for first light so they could make their way to the clinic.

This is life in the lightless world.

My friend loved life without electricity at first, and the peaceful days and long nights helped him and his wife focus on each other, and it wasn't long before she became pregnant. But in time, they both started to feel deprived. The strain of living without power began to overshadow the benefits of peace, tranquility, and star-filled nights. After a few months, they wanted a refrigerator. A laptop. Other conveniences of modern life that would make the pregnancy easier. So they packed up and returned to New York, where Times Square alone burns enough power to light up a small town. My friend and his wife had the luxury of choosing to live with light, or not. Hundreds of millions of people around the world have no choice.

BLACKED OUT ON THE GRID

If you follow the equator from Ecuador to the other side of the earth, you'll end up in Uganda, in East Africa. This country, sadly, is most famous for the bizarre behavior of its former dictator, His Excellency, President for Life, Field Marshall Alhaji, Dr. Idi Amin Dada, VC, DSO, MC, and CBE (the CBE stood for "Conqueror of the

British Empire"), who once said of cannibalism, "It's not for me. I tried human flesh and it's too salty for my taste."[1]

Due to leaders like Idi Amin, who controlled the country in the 1970s, and the deleterious effects of decades of colonization and subsequent warfare, the country has been slow to enter the electrified age. It's a beautiful country, with vast game preserves, forests, mountains, and lakes. But charcoal and wood supply most of the fuel for its citizens' daily lives. Wealthy people and factories rely on diesel generators when the power goes out.

Less than 15 percent of the Ugandan population has access to grid power,[2] which is sad when you consider the incredible potential for hydropower in Uganda. There are a couple of dams on the White Nile, which starts in East Africa and runs through Uganda on its way to Egypt. While some of these dams function well, and there are plans for more, the constant warfare of the 1980s and 1990s critically damaged the country's hydropower infrastructure. Partly as a result of this lack of power and development, nearly 40 percent of Ugandans now live on less than the equivalent of $1.25 a day, much of which they spend on fuel.

Kampala is a teeming city of 1.5 million people, in which taxi motorcycles called motobodas swerve in and out of the city's infamous traffic jams, ferrying people to work and school. It's a city in which high-rise buildings powered by generators stand alongside vast tin-roofed slums, in which families pass evenings in the dark behind walls cobbled together from planks and cardboard. The heat and rain can be oppressive. Much of the city is connected to the grid, but, unsurprisingly, the grid in Kampala is not quite as reliable as the grid in Paris or San Diego. As a result, many people who are "on the grid" sometimes feel like they're off it.

Senguku Ali, a 30-year-old chauffer in Kampala, lives a middle-class life, with a cell phone, iPad, and TV. But on any given day he's likely to be charging his devices in his car, not at home, thanks to the rolling blackouts that plague the metropolis.

"In some neighborhoods it might black out twice a month, and in others once or twice a week," he says.

Lately, he's noticed that some of the wealthier people are setting up their houses with solar arrays, inverters, and batteries so they can be assured of a steady supply. Even though he can't afford these systems, Ali isn't too irritated by the rolling blackouts, since he knows that he's got it good compared to the people in the rural areas of the country.

A CURRENT MATTER

A visit to Mbale, in eastern Uganda, makes this clear. This small city was built on a grid of dusty, wide boulevards and narrow side streets. Some of the neighborhoods have suburban-style homes that wouldn't look out of place in an early twentieth-century California neighborhood. Others are poorer, with shacks and galvanized fences. But no matter the neighborhood, electricity is a constant problem. Some people plain don't have it. And lots of others have a very spotty supply.

Sometimes the electrical utility diverts current from one neighborhood to another, or thieves steal the copper cable from the lampposts. People in Mbale are used to having the lights go out on a dark evening when the kids are studying for an exam, or having their electrically heated shower suddenly go cold when the power dies.

As in many other countries, electricity theft is a problem in Mbale. In 2008, 10 people were fried to death while making illegal connections to the grid. And one man was arrested for running an illegal connection seven full miles from the transmission line to his home outside Budadiri, where he sold power to his neighbors. Regulation is lax, to say the least.[3]

Power in Mbale, as in most of Uganda, is a curious and unpredictable thing. Most curious, perhaps, here and elsewhere in Africa and the low-income world, is the tendency of power companies to cut power just when people most need it. The need is the explanation: when the whole community is home after dark, everyone wants power, and there is rarely enough.

I understand how a grid can become overwhelmed by demand, and why you might at times need to divert power from one place to another. Half my job at Duke Energy was making sure we had systems in place to deal with this issue, usually by increasing power from one of the gas-fired plants. But I have noticed that often in low-income countries the power will consistently go off between 7:00 and 11:00 at night, just when people are settling in to cook, clean, bathe, and do their homework. Everyone's aware of the need, so it's almost criminal to cut it off.

In Mbale, the power sometimes goes off for several days in a row. Recently, in one neighborhood, the power was off for three days straight, but nobody noticed the seriousness of the situation for a day or so because temporary power outages are so common.

In Mbale, when the power goes out, the sound of generators fills whole neighborhoods. That means light for households that can afford diesel, but it also means air and noise pollution for all the neighbors. Given the amount of diesel it takes to produce electric power for one house, generators are probably the *least* sustainable way to make power.

But that's nothing compared to what happens in the outlying neighborhoods and villages.

IT GETS WORSE

Leave the beaten path, and you'll find vast swaths of the countryside in which people get by without any electricity at all. Nearly 5 million Ugandan households use kerosene candles or lanterns for light. These lanterns, called *tadooba*, are dangerous, dirty, and expensive. A recent survey of Ugandan households found that the average family spent two to three dollars a week on kerosene.[4] This, in a country with a gross national per capita income of only $510. Many households easily spend a quarter of what they earn on kerosene.[5]

Drive down Mbale's dusty main thoroughfare into the Bulambuli district and you'll be impressed by the mountain scenery and the small villages and farms. But, sooner or later, someone will mention that the area is notorious in Uganda for rumors of cannibalism. It's said that if you get lost and ask for directions on a dark night you'll be sent down a dead-end road to be kidnapped, killed, and eaten. On one hand, there's no disputing that Uganda has a history of cannibalism. On the other hand, I think these stories are just evidence that people are—understandably—afraid of the dark.

People certainly scramble to get everything done before the sun sets. Everywhere, people are working hard to complete their business. Huge stems of green cooking bananas hang off the sides and rear of bicycles as men in worn suit jackets deliver their goods down the road. Others ride with tall bags overflowing with sweet potatoes or cassava roots. Women in colorful cloth wraps walk with five-gallon jerry cans of water or wicker baskets of goods balanced on their heads. The only people taking a break, it seems, are the kids at play in the dirt in front of mud-brick houses, looking up to stare when a car passes.

Turn onto a back road leading up the nearby mountains. The road is rutted and rocky, with deep switchbacks on the climb to the top. You pass startlingly plain and poor villages of wooden shacks, with concrete block stores selling phone cards, carrots, unwrapped meat, and mobile banking services. The road is red dirt; it bleeds into the dirt yards and walking paths of all the buildings. Electric lines don't make it to the top of this mountain—it's too far, too expensive, with very little payback.

Everywhere, people go about their business in the pervasive red dust. In some villages you'll see a group of men hanging around a table, playing betting games and drinking the local brews. These villages are often uninspiring and unwelcoming even in the daylight—and even more unwelcoming at night. There are few opportunities to start a business or improve one's life. People are forced by circumstance to exist from day to day. No doubt, many would be glad of more long-term opportunities.

I've traveled around the world many times over, and I've seen a lot. But I'm an American, raised in comparative luxury. My childhood was one of clean water, bright lights, TV, and various kitchen appliances. As an adult, I've never lacked for much; I've even been pampered. I believe that Americans—and Europeans and Canadians—have lost perspective on the incredible conveniences our riches allow us to take for granted, things like light switches; good, easy transportation; clean tap water (even imported bottled water from distant glaciers, or South Pacific atolls); and endless hot water to clean ourselves. But anyone who sees these villages, and understands that the people in them probably have no expectation of ever living somewhere else, will be humbled. The people here deserve light as much as any of us. They deserve radio and TV news. They deserve the basic resources that will enable them to go about the task of improving their lives and to give their families a fighting chance at succeeding in a very harsh world.

At the top of the road, 1,500 feet or so above the valley floor, there is a village of about 50 people. This place seems to be the very picture of an African paradise, with banana trees, bright sunshine (broken by the occasional pounding rain shower), flowering trees, and an incredible view for miles. The houses are well kept, made of mud and wooden posts, with whitewashed exteriors and rustic interiors lit by small windows. The ceilings are mostly made of corrugated metal. A group of villagers gathers in a small church to talk about how the need for electrical power has affected their lives.

"You know, several local kids have died from coming into contact with illegal electric wires farther down the mountain," says one woman wearing a purple head scarf and a striped red and orange shawl. "But up here, the problem we have is with kerosene."

The villagers talk about how their babies get painful, red eyes from the kerosene smoke, and many say they think it's affecting the kids' eyesight. Most frightening is that each person knows at least one other family that has lost a house, and sometimes children, to kerosene fires.[6]

A TRAGIC FIRE

Across the border from Uganda, in Tanzania, 9 out of 10 people also rely on kerosene for most of their light.[7] In fact, cross any border in Sub-Saharan Africa and the story will be the same: kerosene rules.

Raphael Robert was 14 years old when he learned firsthand just how harsh kerosene can be. Raphael grew up in Dar es Salaam, the largest city in Tanzania. His home had no power, and his family used kerosene lanterns for light.

"None of us kids had electricity at home. Yet in primary school our teachers were always giving us homework to do at night," he chuckles. "I never understood it."

He couldn't afford to continue his education after primary school, so he hit the streets selling peanuts and donuts to help his family out. His future looked monotonous and bleak. A year after leaving primary school he was fortunate enough to be sponsored to attend a church-run boarding school on the other side of the country, near Mount Kilimanjaro. He was very grateful for the opportunity, since he would be the first person in his entire family to go to secondary school.

"It had been really tough. I'd been working on the street for a year, and this school was a way out," he says.

Every evening he would join several hundred other students to study in a huge hall that was lit by just one large kerosene lantern hanging from the ceiling. That worked fine for those in the center of the room, but for students farther out there wasn't nearly enough light to read by. Frustrated with how difficult it was to study, one boy made a kerosene lamp out of a can and a wick—a do-it-yourself option that many people use in their homes. All the boys slept on bunk beds in one large room, and one night he set the lamp on the wooden bar at the end of his top bunk and studied while the other boys slept. But then he, too, fell asleep, with the lamp still lit. As the boy tossed and turned in his sleep, the lamp fell onto his mattress and started a fire.

Since there was no glass in any of the room's windows, the smoke blew outside, and no one woke up until the fire was raging through the open dormitory.

"I woke up to the sound of people screaming," Raphael says. "They were crowding into the doorway to get out."

Eight boys died that night, and the dormitory was destroyed.

"I knew all of them," Raphael says.

Now Raphael lives in a house in Arusha, Tanzania, with his family. They have electricity, though many others in their neighborhood don't. Last year two neighbor boys fell asleep while studying under the light of a candle. Their mattress caught on fire and the two boys died.[8]

POISON LIGHT

In Sub-Saharan Africa, people pay, on average, 600 times more for each unit of light produced by kerosene than they would for incandescent lamps powered by a grid. The light is terrible.[9] And it's toxic.

Kerosene doesn't evaporate cleanly. Sometimes a bit of it will spill on a woman's hair as she carries a can of it on her head up a rocky switchback to her village. It leaves a smell, and can sting the skin. The fumes are awful, and greatly increase the risk of bronchial infections. Kids who sit down with a kerosene lamp to study often start coughing within minutes.

The fumes are irritating at best, toxic and disorienting at worst. Kerosene is sometimes called a "silent killer," and indoor pollution from kerosene is thought to contribute to 1 million deaths worldwide each year.[10] According to the World Bank, repeated exposure to kerosene fumes is as unhealthy as smoking two packs of cigarettes a day. On top of that, a recent study at the University of California (UC) Berkeley found that women who used kerosene lamps at home had a 9.4 times greater rate of contracting tuberculosis than women who didn't use kerosene for light.[11]

"Getting rid of kerosene lamps may seem like a small, inconsequential step to take, but when considering the collective impact of hundreds of millions of households, it's a simple move that affects the planet," said Nicholas Lam, a UC Berkeley graduate student in environmental health sciences, who was the lead author on one of the studies.[12]

In addition to these dangers, kerosene fumes contribute to climate change: a family using kerosene releases about 300 kg of carbon each year.[13] Another UC Berkeley study found that about 9 percent of the kerosene burned in wick lamps turns into black carbon when burned. That's about 18 times more of this super-destructive byproduct than is produced by burning wood. According to a report by several scientists in the journal *Environmental Science & Technology*, one kilogram of black carbon contributes as much to climate change as 700 kilograms of regular carbon dioxide over a 100-year period.[14]

It's said that black carbon from kerosene lamps in Africa right now causes more climate change than all the CO_2 released in the UK.[15] But scariest of all, perhaps, is that fires caused by kerosene lamps today kill untold numbers of people every year.

The excerpt below from *The Times of India* reports a story that is very typical in the low-income world:

KOLKATA: Two children, three-year-old Jhumpa Mandal and her one-and-a-half-year-old brother Vivek died after suffering severe burn injuries at Kultoli's Jalaberia village in South 24-Parganas late on Friday. Their mother Draupadi, 24, too, has been admitted at a nearby hospital in critical condition.

The tragedy occurred after a kerosene lamp overturned inside their house. The lamp toppled onto the floor after Jhumpa accidentally touched it. The fire spread rapidly inside the house and both Jhumpa and Vivek suffered severe burns.

By the time local villagers rushed in to their rescue, the two children had died. Their father Rabi Mandal, a labourer, was not in the house at that time. Draupadi was rushed to Jamtala hospital in critical condition.[16]

UNABLE TO STUDY

These accidents happen wherever there is no electricity. In India, hundreds of millions lack access to electric power. And hundreds of millions more have limited access, with frequent prolonged blackouts that make their lives nearly as difficult as those who lack power altogether.

Sharma Rakesh grew up in a village in the state of Bihar, India. When he was a child the government invested in grid infrastructure for his village and others nearby, hoping electricity would bring the pastoral community into the twentieth century. But then in the 1990s a terrifying monsoon swept through the area, knocking down power lines and flooding equipment. The electrical power went down and it never came back.

Because there was no electricity, Rakesh grew up using kerosene lamps, which made it impossible to study. He didn't complete school. He lives in New Delhi now, but his mother still lives in the village. Lots of young people have left, and those who remain continue to live in the dark once the sun has set. They have no expectation or even real hope that electric power will ever return to their lives.

Cross the state line from Bihar into Uttar Pradesh, and you're in the most populous state in India, which is saying a lot. If it were its own country, UP, as it's known, would be the fifth biggest country in the world, following China, India as a whole, the US, and Indonesia. UP has around 200 million people living side by side, with a density of over 820 persons per square kilometer. By comparison, the United States holds an average of 34 people per square kilometer. Only a little over 60 percent of the UP population has access to electricity.[17]

This explains why, when you travel in Uttar Pradesh, you are never out of sight of other people. Heading up a potholed road through the rice fields and wetlands outside of Raebareli, in a landscape devoid of towns or very many visible villages, you'd think you were driving through a quiet rural area—except for the people on bicycles who form an endless line along the side of the road, and the people walking in sandals, and the kids playing in the irrigation canals, and the men defecating openly in that same water.

As you travel down this small but crowded road, you will see a huge electrical substation on the left, which makes sense, because a little way farther down, on the right, is a massive railroad car factory. This complex, the size of a Chrysler plant from the golden days of Detroit, needs huge amounts of power. This is unfortunate for the people who live outside Raebareli and compete for that same power.

A MEDIEVAL LIFE

A visit to the nearby roadside home of Ramnarayan Jaheb Bin gives you a glimpse of life in the dark ages. He's a 60-year-old farmer who wears a traditional grey kurta. He rises to greet you from his perch on a wood and woven grass bed parked in the dirt in front of the house he owns, which is home to 19 extended family members. Several other men lounge on beds nearby—it's evening, and they're resting in the cooler night air after a day spent in the fields. A group of women occupy some other beds a few yards away. As is so often the case in India, the women and men don't mix it up much, especially outside the home, in front of strangers.

Mr. Bin guides you inside the maze-like mud and brick home, which has a dirt floor and almost no furniture. The small rooms are lit only by the light from tiny windows and the gaping front door. It is so dark in the late afternoon that you're surprised by people who seem to pop up out of nowhere, or stand silently in a dark corner, or lie motionless on a stone bed in the shadows, following you with their eyes. Mr. Bin's wife emerges, covered in a veil, from a pitch-black room. Near the open-air kitchen in the center of the house, a room is lit with a small kerosene lamp. This is all the light, for 19 people, including a bunch of children.

The kitchen ceiling has a large, minaret-shaped opening that lets light and air in, and the smoke from the cooking fire out. It is the most pleasant room in the house, at least for now. Once the sun goes down, the mosquitoes will invade, and the only light will come from the flicker of the smoky kerosene lamp.

"My kids can't study with this light," says Mr. Bin. "It's just dangerous and dirty. I would like my grandchildren to be able to finish school," he says, sitting in the darkness that would never allow a kid to read or do equations. "Clearly, electricity is a basic human right that we don't have."

The lack of this basic right is clear when you leave the village after dark. As you drive along a dike separating two massive rice paddies, the headlights catch a glimpse of color ahead. As you get closer, you see a group of three women disappearing into some bushes along the wetlands. They left their homes in order to perform their basic bodily functions in the bushes around the rice paddies, because they have no toilets. They've walked out here in the dark, without benefit of flashlights or even candles, as they do every night. The headlights have surprised them. But maybe the light will help scare the snakes and other animals that plague these women night after night as they go about their business. Driving farther toward the main road, the headlights shine on several other groups of women who've come out into the night for the same reason. They look embarrassed and afraid. It's not easy to live well in the dark.[18]

There must be a better, brighter way.

3

FROM THE COAL MINE
TO THE COFFEE POT

THE ALARM GOES OFF IN THE DARK, THE DIGITAL CLOCK blinking red and the radio blaring traffic talk and pop. The bright light illuminates every flaw as you brush your teeth: one minute on the top and one on the bottom, and then the electric toothbrush beeps to tell you you're done. Ahhh—the inviting aroma from the coffee pot that's programmed to kick in on its own every morning. That coffee would go well with toast and jam. You descend the stairs, hungry. Put a few slices of bread in the toaster, push the button, and watch the metal coils turn red to heat up the bread.

"Don't you ever stick a fork in there if the toast gets stuck. Goodness gracious sakes alive, you'll get electrocuted!"

It's your mom's voice, from long ago. Crazy, but that crosses your mind every time you make toast. The toast pops up, perfectly browned. For a second, maybe just a nanosecond, you think, "Amazing. Where on earth does all this power come from?"

That's a really good question, and one I think we're going to be asking more often in the coming years, as our need for power and our sources of power continue to evolve.

Since 1980, both the US and the world at large have doubled their electrical use. That's because many more people are making toast, storing digital info on the cloud, and using robot vacuums.

And worldwide usage is expected to double again in the next 15 years. That's a staggering figure.

The coal-fired generators needed to meet this demand would release massive amounts of carbon into the atmosphere at a time when most scientists predict climate change disaster is looming, if not already here. As for nuclear power saving the day, when you consider that it takes a good ten years and $15 billion to build one nuclear plant these days, and that there's still no clear-cut method for disposing of nuclear waste, it seems unlikely that plant construction could keep pace with demand. I'm by no means saying we need to stop using coal and nuclear power; I am saying that we'd profit from a clearly articulated vision of how the future of power is going to work. And we'd better start implementing those plans soon.

ELECTRICITY IS CENTRAL
TO PROGRESS

Adding to the urgency are the pressing needs of the nearly 3 billion people worldwide who use wood and kerosene and other fuels like dung and trash for at least part of their household energy.[1] This tremendous need is pretty far off the radar for most of us in the West. However, like us, those without electricity would like to charge cell phones, read at night, and have fans in the summer. Electricity is central to the progress of any modern society. It might even be the most important element.

If you're skeptical, just consider all the facets of modern life that depend on electricity, beyond simple things like refrigeration and cooking. There's Wall Street, which is propped up entirely by electronic trading. There are microchips that influence everything we do. Medicine. Education. Communication. And light.

Oh, yes, light. That convenience we take for granted, that everyday luxury that lets us read the paper in the morning, examine our wrinkles—or lack of them—in the mirror before heading to bed, and that lets us complete all sorts of tasks and pleasures in the hours in between. That luxury that lets doctors research our symptoms and figure out a cure. That helps the artist finish her canvas. That lets the point guard see just where to put the ball so it swishes through the basket. It's just there, a given—until the power goes out. And when it does, we feel a bit panicked, sometimes even hopeless. Just ask the victims of Hurricane Katrina, or Superstorm Sandy.

Believe me, I'm not immune to the habit of taking power for granted. Most of the time, I'll switch on a light, or plug in my phone, and not give it a second thought. And I was the CEO of a power company!

But once in a while I'm mindful enough to pause for a moment to consider the marvel of what is really happening when warm light fills the room. To think about exactly where that electricity is coming from, and how far it has traveled. Electric power is a beautiful manifestation of just how mysterious our universe is. And it boggles my mind to think of how long that energy was stored in the ground before we turned it into power.

LOCAL COAL

As a boy, I was intrigued by a small metal hatch on the side wall of our home in Kentucky. Whenever I could, I'd open it and peer down the sheet-metal chute into the dark cellar. This was where the coal man would deposit the coal that we would burn in the fireplace to supplement our gas heat on a cold day. Looking into the dark basement, I wanted to slide down the chute—I mean, what nine-year-old boy could resist? But I never did, because my mother would have killed me when she saw the dust on my clothes. Local or not, coal's just not that clean.

These days, there's a lot of talk about local produce, local meat, and locally roasted coffee. Well, back then, we were burning locally mined coal to heat our home, using energy that had been stored underground for millions of years.

Our house was a nice middle-class house, and so were all the others in my neighborhood. Yet many of them burned coal. It's just the way we did things. I can still picture the small, uniform nuggets of black bituminous, and the blue and orange fire that to my young eyes seemed as intense as the flames of Dante's inferno. Those black chunks were energy from the past, I knew. And it amazed me how we could take that stored energy—what scientists call "potential" energy—and turn it into real, live, warming heat.

Any physicist will tell you that there is a finite amount of energy in the universe. It was here at the beginning, and I guess it will be here at the end. You can't create more, and you can't make any of it disappear (though it will disperse into the world if you convert it or use it). The total never changes. It just changes form. For instance, when you burn a piece of wood in a campfire, you are releasing energy that was previously in the tree. And that tree, in turn, was storing energy from the sun, and the earth that fed its roots, and the water that fell on its leaves. And when you burn the wood you convert it to heat energy, in the form of flames, some of which is absorbed by your body, to warm you, and some of which goes up into the air. The finite amount of energy in the universe is always on the move, from here to there. In a sense, you never "waste" energy. You just don't convert it well.

We humans have become pretty good at harnessing this energy for our own comfort. Think about what happens when you play a Bach concerto loudly on your stereo. That beautiful sound is the product of energy that went into the original recording and the electrical energy that's being used to play it in your living room. And when the notes end, the energy is "gone." Once you've "used" it, the energy assumes another form. Likewise, every time you "add" energy to something, such as when you charge a battery, you are taking energy from somewhere else and putting it to your purpose. It's all a big push-me-pull-you. And it's all a miracle.

KEEP THE RURAL POOR IN MIND

If you live in the high-income world, electrical energy is pretty much a given. It's in the background of everything you do. As noted, in the low-income world—especially in rural areas—regular electricity is nothing more than a wish. The result is that a huge proportion of the world's population is far from the modern world, and getting farther.

I try to keep the rural poor in mind when I think about power. First, I feel grateful for what we have here in the United States, which became nearly fully electrified back in the 1930s and 1940s, under the federal government's Rural Utilities Service. And second, I feel obligated to help bring electric power to those around the world who don't have it. But I hope to find a new way to deliver it that doesn't involve the heavy pollution of power plants, or the complex grid of electrical wires.

It's very clear to me that the system of electrical power we have in North America and Europe, which is now being instituted in much of China and India and elsewhere, is not sustainable for the future of the planet. So we're going to have to figure out something else, and soon.

HOW IT CAME TO BE

The first step toward a solution is to understand how electricity works.

Our modern electrical grid began in 1882, when Thomas Edison flipped a light switch at the JP Morgan Bank to light its offices in lower Manhattan. Just imagine how eerie nighttime Manhattan would have been in those days, lit mainly by flickering gas lamps, kerosene, and candles. And how dark the offices must have been during the day, with only light from windows to fill the rooms. The switch also lit up a few dozen bulbs at the New York Times building nearby. These weren't the first lightbulbs ever lighted. But they were the first to light up according to Edison's idea of "subdividing" power, so that it could be funneled into private homes, businesses, and the like. This power was generated at the nearby Pearl Street coal-fired generating plant.

I've always been amused by the fact that banking and media were the first groups to receive Edison's electric light, because they've been exploiting it and complaining about it ever since. As Edison learned, no good deed goes unpunished. Within a few years, Edison's direct current (DC) system gave way to Westinghouse's alternating current, or AC, which used high-voltage current to let the electricity travel longer distances. Later, Samuel Insull, a disciple of Edison's, led the electricity supply business into the twentieth century, and helped it become a monopoly business regulated by the government, with costs paid for by the customers.

In America, electricity comes from several sources. The most common source is the local power plant, which generates electricity by spinning turbines with steam that's been heated by natural gas, oil, or coal, or some combination of these three. There is also hydropower, in which the turbines are spun by water. And there is nuclear power. And there are wind and tidal turbines, and solar power. But coal is the main source of the electricity that keeps our food cold, sends our text messages, and pumps our drinking water. It's a long and complex path from the coalfields to your morning coffee and toast. We'll start at the beginning.

About 300 million years ago, way before the dinosaurs, the earth was covered with fertile swamps filled with giant trees, massive ferns, and other plants. The oceans were filled with plant life too, mostly soupy algae. This is called the Carboniferous period, because it was the time when carbon was compressed into oil and coal. When the plants and trees died, the woody material sank into the swamps and oceans to make peat, the waterlogged, spongy material you find to this day in bogs. In time, the peat was covered up by other materials, such as clay, minerals, and sand. Bacteria wouldn't grow in this compressed mix, due to a lack of oxygen, so the rate of decay was incredibly slow. Eventually, the sludge dried and became sedimentary rock. As the heavy rock layers grew, the peat was squeezed dry, and superheated, and over millions of years almost every element diminished but carbon. The pressure turned the organic peat into carbon fuels such as coal, oil, and natural gas. It probably took about 10 feet of peat to make one foot of bituminous coal in Eastern Kentucky.

COAL CULTURE

Some people estimate that the US has enough coal underground to last another 250 years, and for that reason the US is often called the "Saudi Arabia of coal." Most of the coal is found in Kentucky and West Virginia, Pennsylvania and Ohio, and Montana. It's also plentiful in India and elsewhere in the world, with China holding huge reserves of coal, though it's not quite as high quality as that found in America. (These days, the Chinese burn so much coal that they import supplies from the US.) Getting it out of the ground can be a brutal and environmentally destructive proposition.

Open-pit coal mines are huge cavities dug out of the surface of the earth that can scar large amounts of landscape for coal removal.

With underground mines, tunnels are used to reach the coal. Miners in trains called mantrips descend through low tunnels deep into the mines, sometimes as far as two miles. There, machines called "continuous miners" dig tunnels and mine coal at the same time, in an endless loop. Miners ensure tunnels are shored up with metal rods and other devices to prevent collapse. Coal is also harvested in a very destructive practice called "mountaintop removal," in which the tops of mountains are literally scraped off to get at coal underneath. The process leaves a barren scar and sends soil and rock downhill, ruining streams and hillsides throughout Appalachia.

The men (and it's nearly always men) who work these mines often come from families that have worked the coal for generations. It's deep in the soul of their communities. They have coal parties and coal beauty queens. Coal festivals and coal parades. The workers often leave the mine covered in black dust from air so thick they can't see their hands in front of their faces.

The coal is loaded onto railroad cars, for transport. Each bucket car can hold around 100 tons of coal. Some trains link over 150 of these cars. Pulled and pushed by powerful diesel engines, these trains can be well over a mile long. Seeing one in the distance crossing the golden Montana plains is a magnificent sight.

But just as these massive loads are a testament to man's ingenuity, they're also a reflection of our self-destructive nature. Coal is dirty. There's no way around it. While train transport is a relatively responsible way to transport goods, each coal car loses hundreds of pounds of coal dust into the air on its journey.[2] And then there's the diesel fuel that's burned to power the train. And that's just the carbon that's released on the way to the generating plant.

To me, it's remarkable to imagine that this energy, which came from the sun hundreds of millions of years ago and was buried in the ground, is now rolling along the high western plains in a coal hopper, headed for a generating plant that will produce electricity for thousands of homes.

BURNING IT UP

Every generating plant has the same purpose: to convert fuel energy—chemical, atomic, or thermal—into electric power. Let's have a quick look at one generating plant, called Fiske, in a low-income neighborhood in Chicago. In one year over a million tons of coal will be loaded onto trains and sent to the Fiske station, about a five-minute drive from the high-rises of downtown Chicago. The train car comes to a stop near a high mound of machinery housed in galvanized steel just outside the main plant. The lead hopper car is uncoupled and rolled inside a huge gyroscopic contraption that clamps onto the car and actually spins it upside down to empty all the coal out of the box. (Some modern coal cars have hatches that open from the bottom, letting all the coal drop into a chute.) The coal is moved by conveyor belts and earth movers into huge mounds—up to 15 stories high—for storage. There might be layers of bituminous, anthracite, and lignite coal in various shades of grey piled outside the power plant, like a buffet of burn options for the plant operators to choose from. What gets burned depends on how much heat is needed at a given moment. And that is determined by demand and by the availability of electricity from other generating plants on the grid—coal, nuclear, gas, wind, solar, and hydro.

To make electricity, the potential energy in the coal has to be released with fire, transformed into steam, and then converted into electricity. The process is pretty straightforward. A conveyor belt takes the coal inside the generator plant, where it is broken into fine bits, for hotter burning. This pulverized coal is then mixed with air and blown into one of the huge fireboxes the size of a small house, where it burns red and white flames, reaching temperatures of two to three thousand degrees. Large water pipes run through the firebox, heating the water until it boils. The resulting steam, still a remnant of the sun's energy sequestered in underground coalfields for millions of years—is directed at the turbine blades.

These turbines can look like propellers on a ship, or like the spinning insides of a jet engine, or like a steel paddlewheel. The steam hitting the blades spins the turbine driveshaft. This driveshaft in turn spins a turbogenerator, a spinning shaft wrapped in wire and surrounded by a giant magnet, and this is what creates the electricity that the Fiske plant distributes to Chicago.

A British scientist named Michael Faraday discovered the principal of "electromagnetic induction" in 1831, when he found that if an electrical conductor such as copper was passed through a magnetic field, electrical current would be induced in the conductor. When the turbine turns the shaft, the interaction of the wire and the magnet convert the mechanical, moving energy into electric current. Electric current is actually created by the movement of electrons. The current itself moves much faster than the actual electrons.

In a modern generator, once steam has turned the turbine driveshaft, any leftover steam escapes the turbine and enters a cooling tower where much of it is recycled as water that is reheated to make more steam in a partially closed system. These cooling towers sending out white plumes disturb people who drive by power plants, because the plumes look like pollution. But in truth, the supposed pollution is mostly excess steam that didn't get recycled. It looks bad, but it isn't.

Modern coal plants are able to filter out 99 percent of particulates before they enter the air. Though, of course, burning coal still emits very high levels of carbon, especially in older plants with outdated filtration systems. Curiously, it's the invisible particles escaping from smokestacks that are the most harmful, not the white plumes. These days, many coal plants scrub their emissions, but older plants often send tons of toxic waste into the air as miniscule particulates.

The new electric current, which, you'll remember, was once sunlight falling on ancient swamp forests, flows out from the turbine in thick cables that rise up the interior wall of the power plant and connect with the transmission substation. It's still a terribly inefficient process. Energy is dissipated at each stage, and most power plants are only 35 percent efficient, meaning that for every 100 units of energy that enter a plant as coal, gas, or other combustible, only 35 units leave the plant as usable electrical energy. Even more of the energy is lost as it moves over the power lines on the way to your home. This is the kind of inefficiency we need to tackle as we move forward. And sooner than later.

The transformers in the substation convert the low-voltage power (about 25,000 volts) flowing from the generating plant into high-voltage current (about 500,000 volts) suitable for traveling long distances on transmission lines. These long, thick cables are almost always made out of low-resistance metals such as copper or aluminum, because low-resistance materials stay cooler. But that also means that some electrical energy is lost along with the heat as it dissipates.

These ubiquitous electrical lines cross the countryside, supported by giant stanchions every hundred yards or so. These lines are a marvel of engineering, and taking care of them—which is the power company's job—is a huge responsibility. The electrical lines are subject to the normal laws of wear and tear, always fighting off the effects of rain and snow, and—significantly—bird droppings.

A DANGEROUS JOB

People often wonder why birds don't get electrocuted when standing on electrical lines. Well, since they aren't touching any other surface, they become part of the circuit—the electricity just passes through them. But as they stand there, oblivious to the 500 thousand volts, they tend to do their daily business, and the lines and, more important, the insulators that keep the high-voltage power from going down though the stanchions to the ground, get covered with guano. As you can imagine, maintaining and cleaning these lines isn't easy.

I've already mentioned how an Englishman named Faraday discovered a way to generate electricity using wire and a magnet. Well, he also discovered that if a person is fully enclosed in a fully electrified metal container, the current will pass through his body without incident. That principal guides the very brave men and women who maintain electrical power lines. They'll suit up in coveralls that are partially woven with steel threads. They'll grab a first-class seat on a metal platform sticking out of the side of a helicopter and, in one of the most amazing sights around (you can watch it on YouTube),[3] they are lifted up to the lines. There, they touch a metal pole to the 500,000 volt line, drawing a potentially lethal amount of electricity into their bodies and turning themselves and the helicopter into flying Faraday suits.

Thus connected to the power, they clip themselves onto the line with a safety rope and climb from their helicopter perch onto the cables, which are a couple of feet apart. (The helicopter pilots who direct their craft within just a few feet of high-voltage lines also deserve kudos.) Crawling along the cables, with one leg and one hand on each strand, power line workers check for damage and clean off any detritus. This must be done frequently on every inch of transmission line in the country.

Another amazing bit of power line maintenance happens when helicopters fitted with long power saws extending from their sides fly alongside transmission lines, cutting tree limbs that are getting in the way. Given the potential for crashes and electrocution, these are among the most dangerous jobs on earth. All this so you can have toast for breakfast!

IF THERE WERE JUST ONE monopolistic power company in America, electrical transmission would be vastly simplified. But while a power monopoly works well in some other (mostly smaller) countries, the US has many power companies, with some local outfits serving tiny communities, and others, like Duke, providing power to millions of people across great swaths of land.

Electricity will only flow through a closed system, so the power lines allow it to flow out to the end of the line and then back to its point of generation. There is a continuous flow of power through the lines, 24 hours a day, so that whenever you request electricity by flipping a switch, it's there instantly. But the unused power will dissipate quickly.

MOST PEOPLE ARE PRETTY SURPRISED to learn that electricity can't be stored very well. I mean, we all use batteries, right? But large-scale storage is something that's just now being tackled. For instance, Duke Energy has deployed a new form of battery at Notrees, its wind farm in the Texas panhandle. At 36 megawatts, it's the largest battery in the US, large enough to be called a "grid battery," capable of storing huge amounts of electricity. If it becomes economically feasible, batteries like this could transform how we operate the grid. But for now, and probably into the near future, electricity has to be consumed soon after it is generated.

The inability to store large amounts of electricity means that generating plants have to anticipate how much power people are going to need. It's a complex equation. Some types of generators, such as nuclear plants, and wind, solar, and hydro, aren't able to modulate their output very quickly. Once you fire up a nuclear plant, you pretty much have to keep it running. Many people today, myself included, are excited about the potential of wind and solar power to transform the world, but at the moment they face some serious problems. Namely, at some point, the sun goes behind a cloud or the wind dies down. Coal can be modulated. But, of them all, natural gas is the easiest energy source to control.

Individual companies like Duke have a variety of generating plants, which use different fuels running at the same time, to power a given region. The basic, steady flow of energy comes from coal, nuclear, and hydro-power plants that run all day and all night, because they are harder to turn on and off, and they have relatively low operating costs. When demand changes throughout the day, going up or down according to the weather or other factors, oil- and natural gas–powered steam plants kick in, because they're easier to turn on and off. And then at the very peak of demand—when the clothing stores downtown are blasting their air-conditioning through open doors onto the street to draw in customers, when the circus is sucking power at the local fairgrounds, and there's an ice-hockey match in the coliseum—the combustion turbines and backup pumped storage hydro plants are fired up. These plants can be started in a matter of minutes to cover almost any overload.

Duke Energy has a trading floor where traders determine how much power millions of customers are going to need during any given hour, based on many variables. Time of year is a big one—in the summer, air-conditioning can boost usage tremendously. Time of day is another important factor, because late at night the power usage goes way down. There are also many other predictable factors. Something as simple as the Super Bowl could influence power usage: as more people spend more time inside, and more TVs than usual are turned on, more power is used. But then again, demand could remain steady as people watching the game might use their computers and electric appliances less.

Duke is based in Charlotte, North Carolina; when the 2012 Democratic National Convention was held just a stone's throw away from our offices, power usage skyrocketed because of all the TV crews, air-conditioned tents, and other electricity-sucking scenarios. But of all the variables, weather is probably the most significant, with very hot or very cold days raising electricity usage. So all these factors have to be considered when anticipating demand.

To make things even more complicated, most states in the US require power companies to maintain the ability to generate power 12–20 percent above the traditional peak demand period at all times, just in case. That requirement is to help avoid blackouts and other problems. It costs money to keep margins that high, and the customers pay for it with rate hikes, if necessary.

Added to these factors is the unique nature of electrical companies. Like other utilities, including gas, water, and railroad companies, electrical utilities are heavily regulated by the federal government. They've also been granted monopoly power because of the intensive investment required to bring electricity to homes and businesses. Traditionally, utilities were able to pass on the cost of doing business—building plants, fuel and operating expenses—to the customers, while still ensuring the business made a little profit. But more and more the market is being deregulated, which makes it more fragmented. The bottom line is that utilities are required to provide good service, and must get approval for any rate increases. It's an expensive, tricky business to operate.

LOCAL POWER

The final stage of the transmission of electricity begins at a substation near your house. Electricity is diverted off the transmission line and into a transformer that converts the high voltage back into various lower voltages that will be used by factories, subways, streetlights, and also your home.

Somewhere in your neighborhood is another transformer, either sitting in a metal box or mounted on a pole, that steps the voltage down even further, so it can power your 220-volt appliances, such as the dryer and air conditioner, and also your 100-volt household electronics such as televisions, lights, and other devices.

As it enters your home, the electricity passes through a meter. Traditional meters are based on aluminum discs that spin when magnetic fields pass through them—you can see them through the window of your old-fashioned electric meter. Newer digital units also measure current passing over a wire to calculate wattage. Once it is metered, the power goes into a fuse box that can stop the flow of electricity if an appliance or switch has been overloaded or has short-circuited. That way, you won't have fires or explosions.

The power is always in the lines, but it must have a closed circuit before it enters your toaster or lightbulb or refrigerator. You create the circuit by flipping a switch, or pushing a button. When you do that, electricity flows into your device and then back into the wire for the return trip home. When you are done, or the timer on your toaster is finished, the switch flips and the circuit opens and no more electricity flows to your device.

And so, the electricity enters your toaster. The toaster's heating elements are made of a special metal, usually a nickel-chromium alloy called nichrome. This metal has a high rate of resistance, meaning electricity can't easily pass through it, which lets the electrons knock against each other, causing friction. That friction causes heat: thus the glowing red hot metal inside most toasters. In old toasters, the heat triggers a thermocouple that shuts off the power when your toast is nice and brown; in newer models the heat is controlled by a timer.

Your toast pops up. You butter it and spread jam. You sit with your coffee, your toast, and your light and your day begins. It's a miracle, really. That toast was made by energy sent to earth hundreds of millions of years ago with the sun's rays. We Americans are very lucky people. We like our toast buttered, so that's the way we have it.

A VERY DIFFERENT WORLD

Meanwhile, as your day begins, a young woman in Namibia, a sparsely populated and beautiful country on the southwestern coast of Africa, prepares for the end of hers. She knows that soon the sun will set, and before that happens she must bring water from the well to the house and start cooking the mealie pap, made from millet and sorghum, which the family will eat tonight alongside some boiled greens.

As darkness falls, the children gather outside the beehive-shaped home for a quick meal. The sun sets, a candle is lit, and the day ends. There is no chance to study. No hope of communicating. The idea of computers and the Internet may have entered the community, but certainly no one uses any electronics other than cell phones, which they charge in another village. As they say, when it comes to electrical power, the rich get richer, and the poor suffer.

The young mother has only two candles left, and no kerosene for the lantern—the fuel is expensive and she often runs out. To her, the fading light each day is like a threat: be prepared for it, or be dismayed. Darkness falls like a blanket; on a moonless night she has no chance of seeing more than a few feet in front of her face.

Only a third of the people in Namibia have access to electric power. The rest simply do without. From outer space, Africa at night is a vast dark emptiness. Though there are nearly as many people in Africa as there are in China, the continent produces less than 5 percent of the world's electricity. And most of that is used by just a few higher-income nations, such as Egypt and South Africa.

Almost without exception, the only people with electric power in Africa are those living in central cities and wealthy neighborhoods. Huge urban slums go without, or have power only intermittently. Some countries are trying to address the problem: dams are being built for hydropower, and there are grand plans for exploiting the hydroelectric potential of the Congo River. The only problem is that the river runs through territories that are barely governed, and that are covered in impassible jungle. So the grand plans might remain just plans for quite a while.

But maybe this hardship offers a path to the future for all of us. We in the high-income world face incredible dangers from carbon emissions, and the problem shows every sign of becoming worse. Even if the economics worked, the earth just wouldn't be able to handle another billion people burning coal. The problem requires some real forward thinking. Perhaps forward thinking will be easier in rural Africa, where there is little history of electrical supply and demand to get in the way of innovation.

What if we were to create a new grid for Africa, one that was based on local production, small-scale connections, and alternative forms of energy such as wind, water mills, and solar panels? Or, at the very least, what if we could make individually powered solar lanterns universally available, so each family could at least have access to light in the evening, and some power to charge their cell phone?

If the thinkers and doers in cities and villages around the world can figure out how to power rural Africa, and elsewhere, and free hundreds of millions of people from the tyranny of living without electricity, they might also teach us how to better shape our own future.

4

THE INNOVATIVE
SUPPLIERS

DRIVING FROM NEW DELHI INTO THE STATE OF RAJAS-
than, India, you're likely to swerve around herds of beautiful grey
cows headed for the nearest watering hole. As you move through
the crowded roadside villages, you'll see more cows relaxing by the
side of the road, letting the wind from passing cars disperse the ever-
present flies.

If the widespread deference given to these sacred cows isn't
enough to convince you that India is a world unto itself, perhaps
the elephant walking up the highway will do the trick, or the camel
carts, or at least the monstrous steamroller that heads toward your
vehicle in the wrong direction of the passing lane, just because that
route is a little shorter. In India, you quickly learn to get out of the
way and let things happen.

This is on vivid display at Barefoot College, in rural Rajasthan,
which takes a unique approach to providing electric lights to rural
villagers all over the world. In the early 1970s, a young man named
Sanjit "Bunker" Roy bought some land in Tilonia, a couple of hours
outside of Jaipur, hoping to help impoverished villagers learn to install and maintain water pumps that could prevent disease and make
rural lives easier. As the years passed, the simple campus grew into
a large collection of well-made, sometimes dirt-floored workshops,
classrooms, and living quarters spread out over many acres. These

days, rural women from all over the planet come to learn skills needed in their villages, like rudimentary medicine, dentistry, weaving, and—most interesting to me—solar engineering.

Roy and I don't exactly see eye-to-eye when it comes to economics and politics. I'm a dyed-in-the-wool American capitalist and I've spent much of my life creating profits for shareholders. At Duke Energy I had an enormous, high-ceilinged office at the top of a skyscraper, and a private jet at my disposal to travel anywhere in the world on a moment's notice. Though Roy was raised in an upper-class family and was a national squash champion, he now lives and works in a much more modest environment. In keeping with the Gandhian principles of Barefoot College, all the staff members earn the same salary of about $150 a month. They dine together, using their fingers to eat vegetarian food from metal plates while sitting on the floor of the dining hall. All the electricity and light is generated by a sophisticated solar array. It's an egalitarian system, and to tell you the truth, I think it's quite a beautiful concept.

But I'm most interested in the program Roy has established that brings about 140 women a year to the college to spend six months studying how to set up, install, and maintain solar equipment. Many of the women are illiterate, and most have never before left their villages for any length of time. Half the women come from India. The Indians live together in facing buildings along a little lane near the college's post office. The rest of the women, who come from Rwanda, Papua New Guinea, Paraguay, and other distant locales, live a short walk away.

Generally, a local sponsor, such as a government minister, will choose a village for Roy to visit. He and his key associate, Meagan Fallone, will travel to the village and help select the women—it's always women, usually grandmothers—who will come to study in Tilonia. Often, the husbands and other men of the village aren't too excited about the prospect of the women taking off for six months, and Roy and Fallone have to convince them that this education will ultimately benefit their families and communities. Roy is very tall, and he has a forceful way of talking, when necessary, that usually works on tough cases. Put simply, he's intimidating when he wants to be, but he can also be a soft puppy when it suits him.

Recently, a dozen well-respected grandmothers from villages in Papua New Guinea traveled together to Tilonia. It was their first trip on an airplane, and they had to switch planes several times before landing in India and getting a ride to their one-story brick dormitory set on a courtyard a few hundred yards from the central campus of Barefoot College.

Six months later, they were well prepared to return home to their villages and start the hard work of selling the idea of solar power to the community, and then installing solar lighting systems that they would maintain, for a monthly fee. Their months in Tilonia had been a nice break, but the women were ready to see their families and tell them their stories. A few days before leaving, the women gathered in the barren courtyard of their dormitory, and, in the traditional style of their homeland, sang a song they'd written about Tilonia. It had a lilting melody and a soft beat. And the words told the story of one particular hardship: burning themselves by accident while soldering electrical circuits.

"We burnt our fingertips over and over," went the refrain.

They laughed as they finished the chorus.

"Very much worth the scars," said one.[1]

HARDWORKING GRANDMOTHERS

A few weeks later, outside of Kigali, Rwanda, four graduates of a different class at Barefoot College were fiddling with solar equipment in a workshop they'd built with fellow villagers and the contributions of a UK-based charity. These women had accomplished a remarkable feat. All 124 homes in their village, Karambi, are now wired with small solar panels on the roof that feed batteries and transformers, which, in turn, power two to three lights in each home. The four grandmothers, Odette Mukaromongi, Claudine Ubelimana, Cecile Nyiramubandwa, and Dative Mukantabana, brought their skills home from Barefoot College. Using parts from India, the four assembled and soldered together the control panels— a real advantage, because since they made them, they also know how to repair them. And then they climbed the roofs of all the village homes and installed the equipment.

It's a remarkable accomplishment, one that's brought new life to the village homes.

Adelle Ndareyiman and her husband, Peter Dodori, live in a neat three-room home with high ceilings. Before solar, they illuminated their home with kerosene. Now they have a solar panel on the roof, a battery, and three light switches.

"Of course I'm happier with lights," says Ndareyiman. "Anyone would be." Sitting on her bed, one light illuminating the room, she picks up the small, portable solar light that came with her solar system. "And this is good for when I'm cooking, and for going out to the toilet at night—there are snakes here."

She chuckles, but with a face that says snakes are a very serious matter.

Her neighbors are also generally very pleased to have the lights.

But the story of this village also highlights one of the major problems with doing good for free. The cost of the grandmothers' travel to and education in Tilonia was donated by sponsors and by Barefoot College. The equipment used to light the 124 homes was also donated. Barefoot College never intends its work to be a completely charitable project; it does not want villagers to get everything for free. Rather, it hopes the villagers will be able to sustain the costs of maintaining the equipment and paying the technicians. In the case of Karambi, it took months before a single family was willing to pay a monthly fee for the collective maintenance of all the systems. They had believed, incorrectly, that they would pay only the cost of maintaining their individual system.

This caused some problems. For one, the repurposed car batteries that were used to store the sun's power until nightfall were running low on distilled water, which is vital for holding a charge. The entire community needed the distilled water, but no one was willing to take the initiative to collect the funds and hire a truck to pick it up in nearby Kigali. They expected their UK sponsoring organization, the Rwanda UK Goodwill Organization, or RUGO, to take care of it. The acronym RUGO[2] is also the word for "home" in Kinyarwanda, the official language of the country. The organization is run by a British man named Mike Hughes, who works as an adviser to the Minister of Education of Rwanda. He felt it was time for the village to take charge: the usefulness of the entire project hinged on this cooperation. Soon they came together to establish a workable fee and system for maintaining the equipment.

Given their success when faced with a steep learning curve, the technicians hoped to spread their knowledge to other parts of the country. Passing their knowledge on to other villages will be an ideal way for Barefoot College to scale its influence—as long as it works.

ANOTHER VILLAGE THAT MIKE HUGHES proposed RUGO might sponsor was Kageyo, in eastern Rwanda, near the border with Tanzania.

As you leave Kigali headed toward Kageyo, everything looks fresh and modern, with gas stations and streetlights, and a lot of hardworking people clearing weeds from drainage ditches along the roadside. But soon the road splits, and the track to Kayonza district is a dusty road with the occasional bicycle carrying huge piles of what Rwandans refer to as Irish potatoes. The villages along this route are lonely and empty, brick buildings and broad dusty plazas;

sometimes you see a person, looking bone-tired, sitting under a shade tree. Kageyo is at the end of this road, a seemingly fitting place for once homeless people to try to re-create their lives once more.

For decades, Rwandan society has been largely composed of refugees. Some are foreign refugees from countries such as Congo. Others are Rwandans who were forced to flee the country during the genocide, or during earlier troubles, and who have since returned. The group in which RUGO is now interested fled Rwanda decades ago, and established homes and communities in Congo. But in recent years, the fighting in Congo forced them back to their own country, Rwanda. Sound confusing? Try living it. While they are legal residents of Rwanda, in many ways their home is neither here, nor there.

Passing deep into the countryside of Kayonza district, you enter a land of no industry and very little commerce. You drive by several tiny collections of brick or earth houses, too small to be called villages, in which families of subsistence farmers go about their lives far from schools and government agencies. Nearing what seems to be the end of the road, you pass yet another refugee settlement—this one so new, it doesn't yet have a name.

Less than a year before, the government of Tanzania had kicked the villagers out of the refugee camp in which they'd lived for generations and bulldozed all their possessions into the ground. They arrived back in Rwanda with nothing, planning to rebuild their lives yet again. The villagers built these homes just months before, using bricks made from scratch in traditional roadside kilns, and the government supplied their tin roofs. These 50 or so houses, with their early-stage gardens—some with hopeful looking flowers planted in the front—have no electricity. For light, the villagers have to scrounge up enough money to purchase candles. Money is very tight because there is no work here, and no way to get to the next town, except by mototaxi, which is expensive. Solar electricity could be transformative, giving people who can make marketable goods the opportunity to work at night, and giving children a chance to read and improve their lives.

It's remarkable what willing people can do with very little. This becomes clear just two kilometers down the road, where the village of Kageyo paints a much more optimistic picture. Most of the residents of Kageyo were born outside of Rwanda, in camps. And now they are back in their family's homeland with a clean slate. The people in Kageyo returned to Rwanda 8 to 10 years earlier than those in the other refugee village. Kageyo has small stores, cell phone charging stations, agriculture and other small industries, including a women's basket-weaving cooperative. But, aside from a solar array at the area health clinic, and a generator for the phone-charging kiosk, this village has no electricity.

Recently, a group of well-dressed villagers gathered in a room at the clinic to talk about their needs with Consolee Uwibambe, vice mayor of the Kayonza District.

Many of the men wore suits, and the women wore colorful dresses, shirts, or traditional clothing. They were hoping to send a group of women to India to learn how to install solar panels.

"It's important that the villagers contribute their work and also money to have the solar systems installed. They know the electricity will change their lives, and they're willing to do what it takes," said Uwibambe.

One man, Mark Muvunyi, was very eager to get the expertise to install solar lights. "We want to develop as a community," he said, his eyes lighting up. "I'd like to make a small business—my dream would be to have a poultry farm to sell chicken and eggs."

Near him, a woman named Niyibizi Narcisse said she wanted to clean up the air in their houses so the children wouldn't be exposed to so much pollution from kerosene and diesel. All the villagers murmured in assent when Narcisse said many of them passed night after night in their homes without light because candles and lanterns are too expensive.

The group walked to the local school. In front, the community had planted a vast garden, with cabbage, peppers, greens, spinach, beets, potatoes, and mango and lemon trees. It was a lovely place, but also practical, producing crops that could nourish a lot of people. But the garden rows were quite dry, serviced only by a hand pump and a bucket. Solar energy could solve that problem too, by powering a small irrigation pump.

The villagers' simple proposals could have vast impact on this distant community of eager refugees. But just getting the expertise and the equipment needed to put their plans in action—even if the villagers were willing to pay a share—could be a long and complicated process. While the villagers had the will, they still had to convince RUGO to help with their expenses, and they had to convince Bunker Roy and his team to invite them to Tilonia.

The hurdles facing this village highlight how much there is to do in the world, and how little actually gets done. At present, Barefoot College in Tilonia can only train about 140 solar engineers per year, with half of them staying in India after they graduate. Although Barefoot College is working on expanding its campuses to other countries, the college's impact will still be very small in terms of the thousands, if not hundreds of thousands, of villages that could use a team of homegrown solar engineers. Clearly, we have to find a system that will scale.

A GIVEAWAY WITH GOOD EFFECTS

Another village in Rwanda has been helped by a different approach to providing clean, sustainable power. In 2010, Joe Hale—one of my associates from Duke Energy—and I founded a nonprofit called The Global BrightLight Foundation. Since the founding, we have distributed about 60,000 solar-powered portable lamps in Rwanda, Zambia, Peru, Haiti, Uganda, Nepal, Bolivia, and Guatemala. This makes us one of the largest distributors of lights on the planet.

One of our most rewarding projects has been distributing lights to the Kiziba refugee camp, hidden in the hills near magnificent Lake Kivu along the border with Congo in western Rwanda. For this project we partnered with a lanky young 33-year-old American named Sam Dargan, who has lived in Rwanda since he was 19, working in solar energy much of that time. He founded a company called Great Lakes Energy, based in Kigali, which distributes solar-powered lights and is also developing microgrid systems for health care facilities around the world. Dargan has done some very innovative marketing in Rwanda to get solar lamps into the hands of people in both distant villages and urban neighborhoods alike. He's sponsored well-known musicians to write songs mentioning both solar power and the lights he sells, with pretty good results. But it's an uphill battle, as his experiences in Kiziba illustrate.

Kiziba was established in 1996 to shelter Congolese citizens fleeing the violence in that country, on the other side of Lake Kivu. The various rebel groups that have been terrorizing Congo for over 20 years are now called, simply, "the men with weapons." They make normal life impossible. The Kiziba camp now houses about 18,000 people in a 28-hectare town divided into 10 neighborhoods. Each year approximately 600 refugees are resettled from the camp to countries around the world, which doesn't put a dent in the camp's population, given how many babies are born.

In late 2014 Dargan visited the camp to check on the lights the Global BrighLight Foundation had distributed. Nearing the camp, there were many women and children—some tiny kids and some old, old women—along the roadside. They walked slowly up the mountain carrying bundles of wood (twigs, sticks, some smaller limbs) on their heads, or suspended on their backs with forehead straps. There were no men in sight.

"The women and children do all the work of gathering wood and cooking the food," explained Amir Hirwa, a representative from the United Nations High Commission on Refugees (UNHCR) who was guiding Dargan into the camp. According to several people who live in the camp, most of the men don't have vital roles to play, since their traditional role of providing security and shelter has largely been taken from them.

Across the ravine the metal roofs of the refugee camp spread along a mesa in neat geometric patterns. It seemed clear that the camp was located here to keep it hidden from general view. If it were located on the outskirts of Kigali, the whole world would have to pay attention. Now they don't. Out of sight, out of mind.

From the ridge near the camp entrance, the town below looked orderly and well kept, with carefully laid-out neighborhoods of tin-roofed buildings. But once through the gate, which was manned by the UNHCR, a more chaotic urban feeling took over. The main street was packed with people: students in electric blue uniforms, mothers carrying babies, young men in hip-hop styles clustered near doorways, and older men dressed in well-worn suits and hats, standing and talking in small groups—the wise men of the town. Everywhere there were young kids who clustered around visitors, clutching their hands and smiling.

Still, since there were almost no jobs here, or in the area outside the walls, the camp had a bored, purposeless feel to it. The UNHCR gave the refugees enough cornmeal, beans, oil, and salt to get them through the month, and there were a few community gardens for vegetables. This food was the main currency in the camp. People traded their rations for goods, including alcohol, or Rwandan francs, but then came up short of food for their household at the end of the month.

While the camp was completely off the grid, electrical wires linked a few commercial buildings on the main drag. Some native Rwandan entrepreneurs had installed generators, and sold the electricity to refugees who ran businesses in the camp. So there were several phone charging stations, and even a makeshift cinema in a low-ceilinged house where men gathered during the day to watch kung-fu and other fight films.

Just past the cinema there was an open-air market where traders from the outside sold their goods—colorful cloth, suit jackets, kitchen equipment, and other desired items.

Our organization believes that people are more motivated to care for equipment if they have ownership of it. But in Kiziba, this was a difficult proposition. We were more than willing to subsidize the $25 cost of each lamp, which also included a phone charging outlet, but we found that even a one-dollar charge per lamp seemed out of reach for almost all the refugees. So we decided that anyone could earn credit toward a lamp by performing various types of community service, such as planting some trees on nearby hillsides denuded by the refugees in their endless search for firewood, instead of paying cash. But I have to admit that even this model failed: many of the people never planted trees, but we gave them lamps anyway.

This is a huge issue in the quest to light the world. How do you get people to pay for something that in years past would clearly have been given for free by nongovernmental organizations? How do you convince extremely poor people to part with what little money they have—and in return, how do you justify that? And if you donate the goods, will the people value something they receive for free? I believe finding a way to ensure people take ownership of the new technology is a central issue in finding a way to supply sustainable lighting systems to people who need them.

In Kiziba we ended up providing each home in the camp with one solar-powered light and solar panel, as it was quite difficult to control the outcome, and we wanted everyone to have the lights they deserved. Unfortunately, Dargan had recently discovered that one of the batches of lamps, out of the over 3,700 lamps we provided, was defective, and a number of people had trouble with their lights.

"These are the last people in the world I'd want to have this supply problem with—they just don't deserve any more difficulties in their lives," said Dargan. "They've already been so knocked around that they don't need to feel like they are being mistreated once again."

Meanwhile, his supplier was having trouble getting him replacements, and it seemed that many of the refugees with defective products didn't trust him to fix the situation. So they'd taken it into their own hands, which is the way that much gets done in the camp.

On the packed dirt floor in front of the market a man sat under an umbrella repairing the solar panels and lights that had broken. He was self-taught and very ingenious. He also sold homemade power strips, made of hand-stamped plastic that had been heat welded together, for those with access to the generators.

It was inspirational to see this man fixing the lights on his own. Dargan thought it might be a good idea to hire him as an employee, to improve customer relations and also keep the lights running well.

SAFE LIGHTS

Honestly, when we first distributed the solar-powered lights, I thought they were so small that they couldn't possibly be effective. They were my first lesson in just how dark the world is for people without electricity, and just how much even a simple lightbulb can do to change a family's life. The solar kits bring light for studying and cooking, and power to charge a phone, which allows people to do mobile banking and other tasks that are vital to living in the modern world. One of the most powerful effects has been to keep the women of Kiziba safer from sexual assault. I never would have expected this, and it pleases me to no end.

The mud-walled, tin-roofed houses in Kiziba are set on narrow alleyways and streets, with some lanes leading to the 12 public latrines that each serve over 1,500 people. Of course, there are no streetlights, and at night these passageways are dark and forbidding, even with a moon. In the past, many young girls and women were assaulted as they navigated these dark spaces, making the necessary evening trips to the latrine a frightening experience. However, the simple, portable lights we distributed gave many women a degree of safety and comfort. They were no longer in the dark; and if something did happen, they'd be able to identify their attackers. It's made a huge difference in the rate of assault, and in the feeling of security of the women in the camps.

The head doctor at the refugee camp's clinic says that respiratory infections dropped immediately after the lights began to be used. He thinks that might be due to less exposure to kerosene fumes. But, after a few months, the respiratory infection rate went back up, and the doctor is unsure what that means. Still, he's quite impressed with the lights, and the way the refugees have embraced them.

The doctor says that there is at least a 30 percent resell rate with most goods that are donated to the camp, as people trade the goods for better food or luxuries. The lights in the Kiziba camp have been laser-stamped with ID numbers linked to the owner, so we can track what happens to them. Because of this, we know that the resell rate is less than 0.5 percent, and most of these are lights that have been stolen, rather than resold by their owners. That's a pretty remarkable affirmation of the importance of this program.

Joe Hale, who cofounded The Global BrightLight Foundation with me, and spends a lot of time traveling between the nine countries in which we work, strongly believes that it's important for our clients to have skin in the game, by paying for their lights. He finds this project incredibly uplifting.

While I believe in The Global BrightLight Foundation's mission, I also think that in order to bring light to the 1.2 billion, we're going to have to come up with a more sustainable and scalable option that will spread from continent to continent.

SOLAR SISTER

In 2011, Katherine Lucey founded an organization called Solar Sister with the mandate to "eradicate energy poverty by empowering women with economic opportunity."[3] After a 20-year career as an investment banker with expertise in the energy sector, Lucey retired from banking and turned her attention to finding a sustainable, grass roots solution to energy poverty. Solar Sister's model is to train women as sales agents and send them into their communities to show other women that solar systems (and efficient and clean-burning cook stoves) are not only life-changing technologies, but are also money-saving investments when purchased through Solar Sister.

According to the organization's data, the women entrepreneurs can double their household income by selling solar equipment. And the families who purchase the lights have a one-third drop in household expenses because they stop buying so much kerosene. The children of these homes have three more hours in which to study each night, because of the solar light. Solar Sister says each dollar invested in one of their entrepreneurs generates $46 in economic impact.

While Solar Sister operates as a direct sales business on the ground, and works to be as economically sustainable as possible, it's still a nonprofit that relies on donations for much of its operating expenses and impact. So it is a hybrid example—not quite a charity, not quite a for-profit social enterprise—that might just be the solution for the future. Here's the puzzle Solar Sister is trying to solve: how to get solar technology to the people who live in the most isolated communities, those who don't get a lot of visitors or much help from the government for their needs.

Solar Sister was designed to involve the women of these communities in every aspect of solar power, from the sales to the installation. The sales agents create the market and then fulfill it, and everyone who gets solar power helps spread the word. Becca Schwartz, an

American with years of experience in various African countries, and the Business Development Director for Solar Sister, has a background in charitable work for the Peace Corps and other organizations, but she also has an MBA and has a real interest in selling.

"I'm focused on sales techniques rather than the technical aspects of the process," Schwartz said, while driving to a sales call in the Ugandan countryside outside of Mbale. "I believe—and this is what I teach our sales staff—that you begin with a problem. You get people to describe the issues they have living with kerosene lamps for light. You get them to realize what is going on in their lives, first, because when you live with this problem every day you tend to discount it—it is just part of everyday life. Rather than just talk to them about the expense of kerosene, we encourage potential customers to talk to us about the problems they face, such as indoor pollution and fires."

Early on, Solar Sister offered its entrepreneurs credit so they could stockpile solar merchandise to sell to customers.

"We started out on the consignment model," says Schwartz. "We quickly learned that if you aren't a bank, you probably aren't good at managing credit. So we dropped the credit, and lost many entrepreneurs in the process."

It became apparent to Solar Sister that entrepreneurs who had an initial financial stake in the business tended to do better. To become an entrepreneur, women in the Solar Sister program have to purchase 200,000 Ugandan shillings' (about US $70) worth of solar products for resale. The associates set their own resale prices, though Solar Sister has a recommended price for each item.

Recently, Schwartz and Jayne Opitto, the sales manager for Solar Sister in Uganda, visited the region around Mbale, to meet with some staff sales associates and local entrepreneurs. The trip was part of a two-week tour to meet with every employee in the country, assess how sales were going, and offer advice on advanced techniques. Their associates worked in the most remote areas.

"Our core competency is getting into the last mile distribution, getting into the furthest nooks and crannies," said Schwartz.

She was sitting at a table in a small restaurant that was operating with a diesel generator because the grid power for that part of Mbale had been out for a couple of days. Someone had stolen copper wires from the lines, and repairs were in process. Every time the barista ran the blender the lights dimmed, so Schwartz set one of Solar Sister's solar lanterns on the table to fill the space with light.

"Our staff have to be experts at selling," she said. "In the end, it's about value and cost. You get a customer to realize the advantage of owning a lamp. You don't try to 'sell' them. We want our sales people to be solving problems, not selling."

Another issue is that, especially in Northern Uganda where there's been a history of conflict, many people are used to getting things free from aid groups, and they don't want to pay for stuff from outside nongovernmental organizations such as Solar Sister.

"We strive to hit the tipping point, where we'll get a few people to buy in an area, and then that will turn into a flood as people see the value," says Schwartz. "For that to happen, our entrepreneurs have to be people the community will trust."

Schwartz and Opitto spent the next day visiting two sites. For one visit, they drove over an hour up a mountain on a rough dirt road to reach a village church in which a dozen women and a few men gathered to hear one of their sales associates, Ronald Makooba, warm the group up with his first sales pitch. He had brought some samples, but spent most of the hour encouraging the villagers to describe their issues and needs in terms of light. The people had high hopes that the government would eventually run grid lines up the mountain to the village, but they didn't expect it any time soon. They didn't seem to embrace the Solar Sister crew right off the bat. Most sat far away from Makooba, so he had to talk across an empty space between himself and his customers.

Mainly, they were interested in avoiding indoor air pollution and fires from kerosene, and in saving money. As Makooba, Schwartz, and Opitto spoke, the women moved closer to Makooba, and the men—who had been hanging out at the far rear of the small church—came forward and took seats. Clearly, the subject engaged the villagers. Most of them spent money each week traveling by mototaxi to a store down the mountain to charge their phones. A big complaint was that the guy at the store stole the talk minutes remaining on their phones as he charged them. The villagers were also interested in how much money they could save by using solar power instead of kerosene and candles for light. After going through a detailed budget analysis for one of the households, with Makooba and Schwartz guiding the way, community members seemed pretty convinced that they could save 15 percent or more monthly—a huge amount for people who have very little money to begin with. Then a powerful tropical rain pounded down on the church's metal roof, drowning out all attempts at conversation.

Makooba didn't sell any products at the church, but he definitely planted the seed, and made good connections with the villagers. The team walked back up the dirt trail from the church to the road. It was muddy and slippery now, and the midafternoon sun blazed hot. They climbed back in the car, wound slowly down the dirt road to the flatlands, and continued on to a crossroads for a meeting of sales associates in a community center. It was now about three o'clock in the afternoon. The sun would go down in a few hours, and the team had made impressions on a few dozen people, at most, so far this day, with no sales to show for it.

At this second meeting, about 15 entrepreneurs, some of whom had traveled several hours on buses, gathered to learn improved sales techniques from Schwartz and Opitto, with Makooba demonstrating. The entrepreneurs ate up the instructions and also had a good time checking out some merchandise on display. Several of them ended up buying stock to resell in their communities. It was a fruitful hour that ended with some soft drinks and snacks—all in all, a very good day. But, as with many of the social enterprises I admire and am interested in, the ratio of time to results was very small. Given the amount of legwork involved in Solar Sister's work, it seems it would be impossible to bring sustainable electricity to over a billion people around the world. But then again, Solar Sister has had some pretty impressive results. According to their own figures, the organization has over 1,000 entrepreneurs in three countries. All told, over 180,000 families (perhaps a million people) have benefited.

If we could scale that up a thousand times over, we'd be coming pretty close to dealing with the problem.

MAKING SOLAR PAY IN INDIA

In India, a number of entrepreneurial companies are tackling the problem of scale, with some success. In Kolkata, a company called ONergy has tried various tacks to fulfill their goal of improving 1 million lives by 2015 and 10 million by 2022 by providing sustainable, clean power.

Early one morning, Sudipta Dawn, ONergy's general manager for operations and business development, heads out of Kolkata into the West Bengal countryside. He's wearing a traditional kurta and sandals for his day checking up on suppliers and equipment in the villages. The intense urban crowding of Kolkata quickly gives way to a lush countryside of flooded rice fields, forest, and small villages. Crossing a river, Dawn points out the location of a solar-powered irrigation pump ONergy has installed to help farmers get more use out of their land. This is a tricky installation, but solar irrigation pumps are a technology that could have a huge positive impact in the low-income world, where much irrigation is still done by hand.

The company has tried many options for increasing the impact of alternative energy, solar in particular, on the villages of India. ONergy estimates that so far it has affected the lives of 120,000 people by providing solar lanterns, home solar systems (some capable of powering an energy-efficient television), solar streetlights, and other projects such as irrigation and even solar cold storage facilities for agricultural products.

Like Solar Sister, ONergy uses a network of trained entrepreneurs to sell and service its equipment. Some of the purchases are financed by local microlending institutions, such as Bagnan-I Mahila Bikash Cooperative Credit Society LTD, the women-operated bank Dawn is visiting today. This bank sends women representatives into the villages; they are equipped with portable devices that can print receipts for deposits of as little as 25 cents a week. The bank also makes low-value but high-impact loans to village women who want to purchase lighting systems.

ONergy also partners with companies such as TERI (The Energy and Resources Institute) and The Climate Group and with government agencies to help it progress toward its mission. The company always looks to form alliances with local people in the communities it serves, to build trust and to get a more honest perspective on what is needed.

I see this kind of grassroots relationship as being vital for the task of powering the world. It's very labor intensive, and sometimes emotionally taxing, but there's no way around it. If solar energy use is going to scale at the level I'd like to see, we're going to have to figure out a way to get people into the field, even to the most remote places.

ONergy looks at the world of energy with a new lens, which could help all of us in the near future.

"I think we are moving from a postindustrialized style of production to something new here in India," says Dawn. "We need to think about how we can avoid imposing the postindustrial tools of the West on this new landscape, which is huge. It's like when the cola companies switch to healthier drinks—a new, unexpected change that seems obvious once it's in place. Right now we are in a polarized space between old industrial ways and new thinking. The cost will be high but there's no point in complaining about it—that's the way it is. The world has enough money to fund it."

Although the grid penetrates many of the villages in West Bengal, the lines are often dead due to rolling power outages. Even when they are connected to the grid, families and farmers don't feel they can rely on it. The villages are lovely places, with solid houses, usually built around or near small lakes where people can bathe. It looks like an idyllic life, from the outside. But living in a dark house isn't easy.

One of the bank workers, Sunanda Manna, lives in Bangalpur Village with her husband and two sons. She uses her solar light for cooking when the power is out. Her son uses it to study almost every evening, because there's rarely any grid power when people most need it. That's why, not long ago, ONergy raised the money to install some solar streetlights in the village. The lamps can store enough energy to cast light through the evening hours.

Not too far away from Manna's house is the home of Sandhya Maity and her family. She and her husband cultivate leaves used to make betel nut confections, and they also work in the rice fields. Five months earlier they purchased a solar system from ONergy, and now they can run a fan as well as lights. The money they save from not having to buy kerosene helps justify the cost. Maity says she'd like to get an even more powerful system so she can have a TV.

Dawn walks along a cobblestone levee between two flooded rice fields until he reaches the home of Suparna and Debu Samanta and their children. Debu works at a nearby paper mill, and Suparna sews traditional women's tops, called chirudars, out of her home, using a manually powered sewing machine.

When their house had no light, their kids often went to their grandparents' house in the evening because they were scared of the dark. It was impossible to clean the house, or do any sewing once the sun went down. Both Suparna Samanta and her husband earned 2,500 rupees a month, about 100 rupees of which they put away each month in savings.

They borrowed money from the cooperative bank to buy a three-light-plus-fan solar system, and pay 700 rupees a month on the loan. But Suparna is now able to earn an extra 1,500 rupees a month from sewing in the evenings by the light of the solar lamp and with the cool breeze of the fan that was also included in the system. So there's a net positive. And that doesn't include the 2,000 rupees a month they save by not having to buy kerosene. Some of that money has gone into fixing up their house, including replacing the thatched roof with a metal one.

Suparna believes she could upgrade the system to power her existing sewing machine for about 25,000 rupees, and says the increased work speed would help her earn an additional 1,000 rupees a month.

"We also want to add a TV and the power for that, and we will do that after we pay off this loan," she says. "I think electricity is a basic human right in our world, and that people like us are being deprived of that right in many parts of India."

While ONergy hasn't solved West Bengal's problems, by making partnerships with key players it clearly has innovated in a way that is helping people fulfill their basic needs—and rights.

AN INNOVATIVE SOLUTION

An airplane ride and a drive away, in crowded Uttar Pradesh, an interesting effort is underway by Green Villages, a for-profit social enterprise based in Mumbai. Green Villages was founded by Krish Krishnan, who left India as a young man, studied engineering at Cornell University, and then worked in the United States and elsewhere. About 15 years ago he returned to India intent on establishing a clean technology business.

Krishnan comes from a family of noted labor and human rights activists. "In fact," he says, "my family home was always a shelter for destitute women. My family was a bit shocked that one of their children would go into a capitalist business, but I've convinced them little by little of the worth! I believe that the only way any effort to bring electricity to those who don't have it will succeed is if it is economically sustainable. And for that, you need to make a profit."

Over the years, Krishnan has come to believe that giving things away to villagers for free is a mistake. That it's not respectful to the villagers, and they know it, and they, in turn, don't necessarily respect the goods.

"The 'free' part makes it valueless," says Krishnan.

He decided that he would not get involved in making or selling products or distributing them to individuals. He'd leave that up to experts and focus instead on implementing solutions to the problems of lack of power.

Green Villages sets up centralized solar charging stations in a village, and then makes portable lamps available to anyone who wants to sign up and can pay a security deposit. For a small monthly fee, villagers can drop the lamp off at the charging station each morning, and pick it up, full of juice, each night on their way home from the fields. Many of the lamps also include phone chargers. For every dollar villagers spend on charging, they save at least a dollar on kerosene, and get better light that's also portable.

Krishnan's big innovation here was to contract with the India Post, the state-run postal service, which operates an office manned by a postmaster in every village. He has hired some of these postmasters, many of whom work for the state only part-time, to run the charging stations. It's remarkably simple, cost effective, and scalable. He's really on to something.

"The postmasters tend to be well respected and reliable. We have 130,000 of them in rural India that we hope to turn to as we expand. These men are our brand ambassadors, and they are very effective," says Krishnan.

On a late afternoon in the village of Onbeeh, the postmaster, Kunjbihari Mourya, stands barefoot on the roof of his post office wearing traditional white pants and a grey shirt. He points to 25 or so small solar panels, about 6 by 8 inches each, set in a grid on a rack that faces the sinking sun. Wires from each panel have been gathered and fed through a gap in the roof, and continue all the way down to the first floor, where there's a matching lamp for each solar panel, all of them lined up neatly on sheets of newspaper spread out on shelves. Since it's the end of the day, all the lamps are charged. Soon, farmers and children will come in to collect their families' lamps for the evening.

"They're great for studying, and for feeding the animals at night. Each light comes with a little stand," says Mourya.

"It's great for the villagers—they are very happy," he continues. "We would like to expand capacity because even more people have asked for the lamps than have them."

Green Villages services all the villages in this area with a roving staff of four young local men who get around on the rough roads by motorcycle and bicycle. One of the young men stops at Bhasaban, a nearby village. The postmaster, Rakesh Singh, points out a broken plug on one of the lights, and the Green Villages representatives says he'll fix it immediately. Singh projects a certain authoritative swagger in his cotton mardani and striped white shirt, and gives the impression that the system of distribution works perfectly. He says demand for the lights just keeps growing.

"The village is very bright from these lights—it's so much better than the kerosene lights."

A short walk from the post office, along a path strewn with fresh cow pies, Savitri Devi folds laundry by solar lamp light on her covered front porch. Dinner is simmering on a nearby cook stove.

"Of course light is a basic human right," she says.

Krish Krishnan says his business model is both pro-poor and pro-profit. Rather than being in conflict, these two ideals are symbiotic. That's the way I see it also, and I like it.

A TECHNICAL SOLUTION

Around the world right now there are many other interesting entrepreneurial and government efforts to bring electricity to the people who most deserve it. I am unable to mention them all in this space. From what I've seen, many of these efforts are small, and slow to scale. They have a profound impact on a limited number of people. I feel we need to leapfrog this stage in our solar awareness, and figure out how to truly bring light to the hundreds of millions who need it. We need to stop experimenting and helping, and really start doing. Kris Krishnan is doing that with Green Villages. And there's another effort called Off-Grid: Electric, in Tanzania, that I think is poised to make a huge bang.

The company, which is headquartered in Arusha, Tanzania, at the base of Mount Kilimanjaro, was founded by three young Americans who between them had pretty significant experience in Sub-Saharan Africa. The company calls itself the world's first massively scalable "affordable solar leasing" company. This statement is emblematic of Off-Grid: Electric's youthful ambition, emphasis on forward-thinking marketing, and innovative products. I like that combination.

Recently, Xavier Hegelson, the CEO and cofounder of Off-Grid: Electric, walked through the company's clean, brightly lit offices in a leafy Arusha neighborhood. In one room a team of Tanzanian employees was on the phone with customers answering questions, taking payments, and dispatching technicians on service calls. Off-Grid has developed proprietary home solar power systems that require customers to prepay for service and turn off if payment is not received. In much of Sub-Saharan Africa, mobile banking is becoming the most common financial transaction. Off-Grid's customers make a simple mobile money payment to the company via cell-phone in return for a code they enter to activate the solar equipment Off-Grid has installed in their homes. This way, if they have money to buy electricity, they can do it. If they prefer to wait a few days, that's fine also. The equipment will always be well maintained and in place.

This system solves a couple of issues in getting solar electricity to those who lack power. First, since Off-Grid installs and maintains the equipment, the customer doesn't have to worry about warranties or understand how to repair a complex electrical system. And second, while the customer pays a small daily fee for the equipment, which eventually leads to ownership, they do not have to buy the solar equipment up front. This arrangement not only makes solar much more affordable, but reduces risk for the customer: if their solar system stops working, they can stop paying. This aligns their interests with the company's. That makes high-quality solar power affordable and scalable to many more people.

Off-Grid is a very modern operation, with an emphasis on good design and innovative technology. In addition to the proprietary software that lets the company capture and analyze a ton of data to help it give better service, it's also working on new designs for lithium batteries, hyper-efficient appliances, and TVs that will work well within solar's limitations.

Plus, the company is well branded on storefronts throughout Tanzania. It also recruits the best and the brightest Tanzanian students and trains them at its own academy. There's a sophisticated call center for customer service. All in all it's an interesting and professional operation.

Recently an Off-Grid salesman called on customers in a very poor neighborhood on the outskirts of Arusha. First stop, a small general store whose storefront had been branded with one of Off-Grid's logos, much as you might wrap a city bus with a corporate logo. Above the door was one of the company's lights, serving as an Off-Grid advertisement after dark. There was also a light inside. One common problem is that store owners tend to keep the lights off as much as possible, preferring to use the solar power to fuel their for-profit cell phone–charging business. This is the kind of unexpected issue that you only learn about in the field. Off-Grid is trying to figure out how to manage it.

The salesman has sold about 300 solar units, usually three lights with a solar panel and lithium battery, on commission and expects to sell many more. He seems happy with his income. The houses in this neighborhood are extremely simple and cobbled together, crowded and chaotic by American standards. But they are the norm in this and many other neighborhoods across the world. These are the people who deserve light. And now many of these families have it. Some are now able to work at night if they wish. A cobbler fixed shoes under an outdoor light. And a woman nearby was now able to keep her vegetable stand open after dark, and also wake up in the predawn hours to serve breakfast to early morning workers. This was a neighborhood of industrious people, and the light definitely made a difference. It's a great thing.

Of course, now that they have light, most everyone also dreams of more power, in the form of TVs and appliances like refrigerators. Off-Grid is working on that, thanks to some good partners. The company has received over $30 million in investment so far, including support from Solar City, the largest home solar supplier in the United States. Off-Grid: Electric's goal is to power 10 million homes in 10 years. So far, they've done more than 30,000. I predict a healthy future for them. I think we can learn a lot from their methods about how to scale solar around the world.

Just ten years ago no one would have thought that solar power on this kind of scale would be possible. The price of panels was sky high, and people just weren't that receptive to the technology. Batteries were terrible. And there were few cell phones that needed to be charged. Now, all that has changed. Everyone has cell phones, and solar power looks like the greatest thing going. We just have to figure out how to get it to over a billion more people.

5

ELECTRICITY IN
THE WORLD

HAITI IS A BEAUTIFUL COUNTRY THAT'S SEEN MORE than its share of difficulties and disasters, including death squads, earthquakes, disease, deforestation, landslides, and hurricanes. Only one in four Haitians has easy access to electrical power. Still, it's an island full of hope, where students need light to study and nurses need refrigerators to store vaccines. Haiti is full of people with desires just like ours. They just can't fulfill them as easily, since there's so little power.[1]

Despite this, Haitians often exhibit a make-do spirit that helps the country meet its most pressing needs. They are willing to try new programs and new economic partners to ensure needs are met. For example, a program sponsored by the Solar Electric Light Fund recently installed solar lampposts along rural roads to light people's way at night. People can also charge their phones at these posts, which is a real boon for communication, education, and commerce. This kind of adaptation has become commonplace in a country whose traditional institutions are often of little help.

This lack of support was evident in an interesting announcement from the Directorate General of Electricity (EDH) of Haiti regarding broadcasting the World Cup on TV. The agency stated that it wanted to

> inform the general public and its customers in particular of the Metropolitan region, that on the occasion of the 2014 World Cup it will provide in the extent of its possibilities, access to electricity in the hours of sport competitions. Given the amount available on the grid, the Directorate calls for the cooperation of all, to help him in his task by unplugging during the 2 hours of matches, all appliances and household appliances with high energy consumption such as: Refrigerator, iron, freezer, washing machine, incandescent bulbs, dryers, air conditioners, electric ovens. . . . The Directorate also urges people who are rerouting (illegal) to stop this practice which could result in a general trigger on the circuit, preventing all those powered by this circuit to enjoy the games. The Directorate also invites consumers to regularize their illegal connections, and its debtor clients to make the effort to meet its electricity bills.[2]

The announcement, published in the newspaper *Haiti Libre*, was a clear illustration of how dramatically electrical power varies from country to country. Imagine the citizens of London being told to turn off their computers and washing machines so everyone would have a better chance of enjoying the big match. You can't.

A FEW DAYS AFTER READING the *Haiti Libre* announcement, I attended some meetings in Las Vegas. It was late afternoon under a searing July sun; the TV said the temperature was 105 degrees Fahrenheit—in the shade. Curious about what that kind of heat feels like, I walked out of my 67-degree hotel lobby to meet the heavy thud of dry heat coming off the desert. It wasn't so much the heat as the weight of it as I walked that dragged me down. I quickly learned to walk right next to the buildings on the shopping strip, because all the stores blasted air-conditioned gusts out their open doorways to draw in anyone foolish enough to walk around at midday in the Mojave Desert.

To a Martian, or perhaps even a Haitian, it would seem there must be a limitless supply of electrical power in Las Vegas, right? Why else would stores be air-conditioning the desert? Well, in truth, electricity in Vegas isn't that cheap or that plentiful. In the summer of 2014, the Nevada Power Company ordered rolling blackouts for the first time, because temperatures approaching 120 degrees had pushed electrical consumption beyond capacity.

The same thing happens pretty much every summer now in New York City. Con Edison, New York City's main supplier of electricity, issues bulletins that are repeated over the radio and TV, Internet and newspapers, urging people to turn down their air conditioners and to run their electrical appliances only at night in order to minimize the chances of a brownout, or even a blackout, on hot days when everyone is inside running machines to keep cool.

Still, compared to a place like Haiti, most of the high-income world is awash in power. Europeans, Australians, and Americans have plenty of power—for now. The issue for these countries is that many of their grids are becoming obsolete, reliant on dirty coal plants and aging nuclear plants that will need to be replaced in the next few decades. It's a huge issue to which few people are currently paying attention.

It may sound strange, but in some ways, Manhattan is very similar to Port-au-Prince. For one, both need new infrastructure, from the bottom up, that reckons with the environmental and supply issues of the modern world. And both places have a distinct inability to always meet the demand. On the surface, Manhattan seems to have the advantage. But I often wonder whether places like rural Haiti or Congo actually have a simpler task ahead of them—because their infrastructure is so limited, they can invent a new type of electricity network from the ground up instead of having to revamp an older, vast system. When you invent anew, you aren't hampered by outdated equipment and ways of thinking, as you would be in a big, high-income city like London or New York. In the low-income world, there is little to lose in this area, and much to gain. Not so in more high-income societies, which will have to revamp their old systems—a task so large that people prefer to shield themselves with mental blinders.

No matter where you live, the supply and use of electricity is a complex process that influences every aspect of society. On almost every metric—health, economy, education, freedom—countries with ample electricity generally rank higher.

There are many reasons one country might have more electrical power than another. But natural resources generally aren't the deciding factor. Compare the Democratic Republic of Congo, whose powerful rivers could provide huge amounts of energy from hydropower, but which doesn't generate much electricity, to Japan, which has few natural sources of energy other than coal,[3] yet produces huge amounts of electricity. Clearly, economic factors play a much greater role.

Many countries are working overtime to get more electricity, with mixed results. Let's take a look at some key places.

CHINA

China has increased its power output dramatically—from about 1.5 trillion kilowatt hours (kWh) per year in 2001 to nearly 5 trillion today. That makes it the largest producer of electrical energy in the world. The US, in second place, generates 4.1 trillion kilowatt hours now, as compared to 3.7 trillion in 2001. Coming in third is the European Union, which produces about 3 trillion kilowatt hours, up from 2.8 in 2001.[4]

China's rapid economic expansion has happened in tandem with the growth of its electrical supply. In the past, China had a population hungry for food. Now it has hundreds of millions of people hungry for modern conveniences. An industrial base eager to provide these conveniences to both China and the rest of the world has spread electricity to the nether regions of the huge country. In the process, China's skies have darkened.

While China has dramatically reduced the number of people who don't have access to power, it has also dramatically increased its rate of environmental destruction. Even though China leads the world in the construction of nuclear plants,[5] its major source of power generation is coal.[6] China burns half the coal used annually in the world, and produces the most greenhouse gases. The International Energy Agency estimates that China will double the number of its coal-fired power plants by 2040, which would also double its carbon output. It's also building 50 coal-fired gasification plants that will introduce 1.1 billion tons of carbon into the atmosphere. It's unclear how the recent climate agreement between the US and China will affect that plan. The resulting gas will likely be used to generate electricity and to heat buildings, among other uses.[7]

I recently came across a short video on YouTube that purported to show residents of Beijing standing on a gray morning before a large LED screen that displayed a film of the rising sun. The caption said that on some mornings, this LED screen was the only way for Chinese people to see the sunrise. For the rest of the day, I thought about that video. What tradeoffs we have made! It turned out to be a video hoax—the LED billboard was an ad for a travel company— but the fact that I hardly questioned it says a lot. In truth, there are private schools in Beijing that have installed specially equipped HVAC equipment in their gyms to keep the smog out of indoor recess. Some parents in China have been known to personalize face masks for their toddlers. In response, the Chinese rulers have pledged to greatly reduce coal burning, at least near urban areas, by 2017, and increase their research into clean coal technology.[8]

The country is definitely a leader in the emerging technology of carbon capture, whereby the carbon by-product of power generation is collected and stored underground, so it doesn't get into the atmosphere. Still, no one knows yet whether this wildly expensive technology will actually work in a sustainable way.

While China's electricity use booms, many other countries have stagnating or even worsening rates of power use. This is especially true in Sub-Saharan Africa and low-income countries in Asia, which are home to over 95 percent of the people without electricity. In low-income Asia, 17 percent of people do without power. But in the vast area of Sub-Saharan Africa, over two-thirds lack it—a shocking statistic.

INDIA

Most of the people in Asia who lack electricity live in India and Indonesia. Visit New Delhi and you'll see utility poles beribboned with hundreds of electrical wires traveling out to nearby buildings, poles, and equipment. Often, many of the wires are homegrown, installed illegally by nearby businesses and households that don't want to pay the utility company—theft of electricity accounts for losses of $4.5 billion a year in India. Look at these tangles of wires and try to imagine tapping into them without killing yourself. India has an incredibly inefficient grid system. About 30 percent of the 174 gigawatts of electricity that India produces annually just dissipates while running through the wires and transformers, or is stolen.[9] (For comparison, Duke Energy loses about 8 percent of its power to line loss.) Many people aren't good power thieves; every year in India people die from electrocution while trying to tap into wires.

The Indian grid is chaotic and unreliable in the cities, and overall functionality varies from state to state. In some areas, 90 percent of people have access to electricity. In others, only about 40 percent. On the bright side, about one million Indians now get their light from solar power.[10]

Amazingly, despite the fact that about 400 million Indians lack power, the country is still the world's third largest producer of electricity, behind the United States and China.[11] Still, the electrical supply that does exist is far from great. Blackouts and brownouts harm businesses.

Many Indians create, or supplement, their power supply by traditional means: 800 million Indians still burn wood, dung, and plant-based fuels to cook and heat their homes. This means people are breathing in a lot of smoke. The World Health Organization estimates that 1.7 million South Asian people die prematurely each year from exposure to smoke from cookstoves, most of them in India.[12] Good electrical power would reduce the number of deaths. Electrical power would also improve the water supply. India suffers from a lack of drinkable water. Even the few sewage plants that exist are often closed because there's no electricity to run them.

In India, energy progress of all types—including clean, sustainable energy—can sometimes be lost in the sheer scale of the place. There are so many people that a major effort can seem minor. Right now, India gets 60 percent of its power from coal generation, 17 percent from hydropower, and 9 percent from gas. Yet the country is one of the biggest sustainable energy producers in the world: India's green power—from wind, solar, and other generators—is greater than *all* the energy produced by the entire country of Austria. That's pretty amazing.[13]

INDONESIA

Indonesia is a vast archipelago of over 18,000 islands in the Indian Ocean. Nearly 250 million Indonesians live on 922 of these islands, which are spread across great distances. Some of those islands, such as Borneo and Bali, are famous tourist destinations, but most are obscure, isolated places housing one or another of Indonesia's multitude of ethnic and religious groups. It's a hard place to lay down an effective national grid.[14]

It's not surprising that a full one-third of Indonesians have no access to electricity. Most of the people are poor and isolated in rural areas, living lives largely unimproved by modern health care, education, commerce, or the Internet. As such, they embody the central paradox of why it can be so difficult to bring electricity to those who lack it.

Most of these Indonesians can't really afford electricity, because their village economies won't support it. And if they can't afford electricity, who is going to want to provide it? Yet, without electricity, how will they start a business or get a job that pays enough money to afford electricity? It's a classic Catch-22. We'll have to do some novel thinking to come up with a solution.

The government of Indonesia has pledged to bring electricity to 90 percent of the population by 2020, which would mean 15 million households in just five years. Many people believe that creative financing and cutting-edge technologies will be the key. The World Bank estimates the government will have to spend $4.5 billion per year to implement the plan.[15]

There's a saying that the rich get richer, and it applies to electricity as well. Those countries that already have a lot of electrical power also tend to get more when they need it. That's because the modern grid is a scalable thing. And without the grid there can be no scale, at least not with traditional energy sources, such as coal or nuclear plants. The infrastructure of the traditional industrial grid, with transmission lines and transformers we in the high-income world take for granted, would be impossible to replicate in a low-income country today, due to costs and environmental factors.

AFRICA

This definitely applies to Africa, the continent with the lowest power output, and also the lowest gross domestic product in the world. As noted, two-thirds of sub-Saharan Africans are completely off the electrical grid and rely on wood, dung, kerosene, or candles to cook meals and light their homes. But even Africans who are connected to the grid pay several times as much for their power as they would in the US or Europe, and the power they get is often unreliable.[16]

The African grid is divided into several regions, each with quite limited capacities. A map of the continent's transmission lines shows activity mostly along the northern coast, from Morocco to Egypt; south of that, lines run from South Africa to Kenya, and into the Sudan and Ethiopia. The entire center portion of this vast continent has zero substantial transmission lines.[17]

Even though Africa has huge hydro and geothermal resources, incredible sun exposure for solar panels, and lots of wind to power turbines, the entire continent—nearly three times the size of Europe—generates about as much electricity as the country of Spain.[18]

And even the areas within the grid face serious supply issues. Right now at least 25 countries in Sub-Saharan Africa experience regular rolling blackouts, which make it hard to run a factory or any business that requires a steady power supply. And family life is profoundly affected. Home refrigerators are a risky appliance, since food could spoil at any time when the power goes out. Teenagers studying for college entrance examinations might open a book only to close it a few minutes later because it's too dark to read.[19]

According to the World Bank, this unreliable electricity costs African economies from 1 to 4 percent of GDP a year.[20]

Based on numbers for the continent as a whole, the average African uses just 500 kWh of electricity each year, compared to the world average of 2,500 kWh. That's a startling split. But it doesn't tell the whole story.

Consider this: the average person in the US uses over 13,000 kWh per year, or over 26 times the African average. That's a lot of toasters, iPads, TVs, and computers being fired up in America. Is it my goal to get all these devices for the average African consumer? No, I don't think that's realistic at this point, especially if the power is to be sustainable. But neither do I want to deny the people of

Africa's 54 countries access to devices that will make their lives more comfortable and productive, and yes, luxurious.[21] The continent of Africa is emerging as a major source of creativity, industriousness, and innovation. And it could be a huge market for other nations.

For decades there's been a feeling among many people in the so-called high-income nations that we must somehow cure Africa of its ills, as though we were the parent, and African nations were the children. This is an extremely paternalistic view that we must abandon. Africa is poised to lead itself—and us—into a bright future. I, for one, will do anything I can to assist that movement and growth. As a world community we have to band together and offer our ideas, services, and know-how—when needed and desired—to help speed the great changes the people of all the African countries are making happen now. I believe that by 2030, every single African could have power for lights, water purification, and other necessities.[22]

For now, however, the disparity between the high-income world and most of Africa is even more shocking than I've described. That huge split between the average American and the average African consumer of electricity, in which the average American uses 26 times more than the average African uses is a distorted illustration of how energy is distributed and used on the continent. In truth, the disparity is far, far worse. The figures I've cited so far are skewed by the fact that South Africa and the countries of North Africa use a disproportionate amount of the electricity generated on the continent to fuel their vastly more sophisticated and wealthy economies.[23]

In North Africa, most people have access to power. But in Sub-Saharan Africa, only about 30 percent do. And most of those

Sub-Saharans who have power live in South Africa.[24] If you leave these few high-income areas out of the equation, the average African's electricity use drops to 180 kWh per capita, or about 72 times less than that used per capita in the US. In truth, a full 80 percent of people in Africa use less than 1.5 percent of the electricity used by the average American. That's an amazing disparity. And to put it even more starkly, the 850 million people living in Sub-Saharan Africa use less electricity than the 20 million Americans who live in New York State. Think about that.[25]

The disparity within Africa recalls the differences between areas of rural and urban America back in the 1930s, before the New Deal brought power to many who lacked it. That electricity came from fossil fuel plants sending power over major transmission lines to distant locales. It's something that couldn't be done now, given the incredible need we have to reduce carbon output and halt the progress of climate change.

At the moment, coal is the main source of electrical power in Africa, used to generate 40 percent of electricity on the continent. South Africa mines over 90 percent of this coal, and uses nearly 80 percent of it for its own electrical power.[26] Thirty percent of Africa's electricity is generated from natural gas, 15 percent from hydropower, and 12 percent from oil. Cleaner energy, from wind and solar, makes up only the tiniest part of power in Africa. But again, you have to remember that these figures are distorted because South Africa, which has a lot of power output, uses most of the coal, and because the North African countries, which also have a relatively high power output, use mostly gas and oil.

The continent is divided into five distinct electricity grids, with the North Africa grid dominating. There is no expansive transmission and distribution system on the continent for electricity, or for natural gas, so it's difficult for countries that have power to share it. Add to that the vagaries of political upheaval, several guerilla war movements, and civil wars, and sharing of power sources can become quite difficult. Economics is another reason why distribution systems won't be built: most of the natural gas produced in the gas-rich countries of North Africa and in Nigeria is sold to European markets, because those countries will pay higher prices than African nations can afford. There is a lot of coal in Africa, but the world should hope that new technologies enable African countries to keep that coal in the ground, given the dire state of climate change.

Still, we can't expect African countries to just sit tight and not use the resources they have while the rest of the world surges ahead. If we want to help the African nations develop good supplies of electricity, we need to offer that help in the form of sustainable energy intelligence. The African continent has experienced over 20 years of economic expansion, with the World Bank predicting over 5 percent growth per year in the coming years. And as the economy grows, so will demand for electricity. Some estimate the continent will need 7,000 megawatts (MW) more power each year, but until now the most new power generated annually has been about 1,000 MW. And here lies the challenge and the opportunity.

There is sufficient hydropower to meet much of the demand, but there is not enough money to build dams and run transmission lines. For instance, the Inga hydropower site on the Congo River in the Democratic Republic of Congo has the potential to produce over 100,000 MW, but less than 3 percent of that has been exploited, due to lack of resources, and the wars and political disruptions that plague the DRC. This could be a tremendous, and largely carbon-free, source of electricity. In all, the continent uses just 8 percent of its potential hydropower to produce electricity.

If the dams were built, then power lines would also need to be built. It would be a traditional grid, albeit one that would emit far less carbon than, for instance, any grid in the United States. While the World Bank has financed a huge grid project to connect Ethiopia's grid to Kenya's grid, not much else has been done on a large scale.

In ages past, hydropower lifted many European countries out of economic morass. Perhaps African countries will use it to do the same. Still, hydropower is not perfect. It often depends on turbines moved by active river systems, which are more subject to the fluctuations of nature than the more reliable dams on reservoirs. With either method, however, hydropower depends on the flow of water, which can be unreliable. For instance, water levels on Ghana's Volta River were low during the 2014 World Cup, forcing the government to ration power so its citizens would be able to watch the games on TV uninterrupted by power outages, just as was done in Haiti.

Solar power, which is popping up in all corners of the continent, is really one of the best options, because the African skies have some of the highest solar irradiation levels in the world (meaning they get a lot of sun!). Nouakchott, the capital of Mauritania, in northwest Africa, is an example of solar power in action: it gets 30 percent of its power from solar energy. With its use of hydropower, and the wind farms it is now building, in addition to its use of solar, Mauritania is in the vanguard of renewable energy—a light that may help lead Africa into a bright future.[27]

LATIN AMERICA

About 560 million people in Latin America can turn on the lights and fire up the toaster in the morning, if they wish. Only about 23 million people—most of them in very poor, rural areas—can't.[28]

That seems like an insignificant amount when compared to Africa and India, unless, of course, you're one of the unfortunates without power. In Latin America, the challenge is getting electricity to those who are far from the grid, for instance in the Amazon areas of the continent.

Overall, Latin America has an extensive power distribution and generation network.[29] A lot of that energy is pretty clean, compared to the rest of the world. At the moment, over 50 percent of Latin American electricity comes from hydropower. There are many programs in place to promote sustainable energy where it's needed. An example is Brazil's Light for All program, which has set its own mandate of bringing electrical power to every single person in Brazil within the next few years.

Heading further south, way below the tip of South America, you find solid electrical power in remote, inhospitable Antarctica. For years the power has come from generators powered by diesel fuel brought in on ships. Not the cleanest technology for such a pristine wilderness. These days, windmills are being installed, since the continent is one of the windiest places on earth. But that wind, too, can be a problem, as sometimes it's so powerful it can destroy the windmills that are trying to tame it.[30]

There's a lot of electricity being generated around the world. And a lot of unmet demand, too. I know from my years providing electricity in the United States that electrical power is an ephemeral gift. You get it, and then it's gone, and right away you have to make some more. It's not like a car or a diamond, which you can hold on to and value. The task of bringing power to the 1.2 will be huge and ongoing.

Fortunately, the world is already making gains. Huge numbers of people in Bangladesh, Cameroon, Ghana, Indonesia, Mozambique, South Africa, Sri Lanka, and elsewhere have gotten power in the last year. While most countries in Asia and Africa face decades of work to bring power to those living in the dark, there's great news coming out of China, Latin America, and the Middle East. They're getting powered up. If we do things right, most everyone in the world will have power by 2030. Let's make sure that power is affordable, reliable, and clean—my definition of sustainable power.[31]

6

THE DARK SIDE
OF POWER

WHEN TRYING TO DETERMINE WHAT TYPE OF POWER would work well in a given situation, it's best to judge each alternative by three criteria: Is it affordable? Is it reliable? And is it clean? No alternative will get a yes answer for each of the three points. There is always a tradeoff. At the end of the day you learn that there is no perfect way to generate electricity.

I started my working life as a journalist in Kentucky, covering the local crime beat and federal courts, and it was an exciting time. There's nothing like covering the news, because you get to be inside a situation without being part of it. You are an observer with the best seat in the house, but no responsibility for the outcome.

I left journalism in my 20s to study law, and later became the deputy general counsel for the Federal Regulatory Energy Commission. Following that, I became partner in a private law firm, later led an interstate gas pipeline network, headquartered in Houston, and from there was recruited to lead PSI Energy, in Indiana. One of my first jobs was to deal with the aftereffects of a nuclear power plant that had been shuttered by my predecessor. This was the first time I became part of the news.

And it was a good introduction to my later career as CEO of other utilities. I quickly learned that while people love their lights, appliances, and devices, they often don't realize the true costs of power. They don't realize the environmental harm. The health costs. And the societal costs. During my time at Duke Energy I was often in the news, explaining emissions of sulfur dioxide, nitrogen oxide, fine particulates, and mercury, and what the company was doing to reduce these emissions. But one big issue never went away: that electricity generation accounts for about 40 percent of the US emissions that contribute to climate change.[1]

IN MY 25 YEARS as an electrical industry CEO, I was responsible for bringing power to millions of customers, as well as satisfying shareholders. In the process I oversaw the release of hundreds of millions of tons of carbon into the atmosphere. I made decisions that led to the creation of treeless corridors in forested areas to make room for major power lines. There was always a tradeoff. That's because electrical power, especially when it's produced in the traditional ways we've done for decades, has an adverse impact on the environment. There's no way around it.

I did my best to supply electricity responsibly, although many people didn't see it that way. Witness the environmentalists who several times burned me in effigy. Who another time dumped a big pile of coal on my front lawn and put posters on my house saying I was destroying the earth by burning coal. I understand where they were coming from, and I'm sympathetic to their fears about the future of the planet. But the truth is that most, if not all, of the protestors went home to make their dinner and watch TV with electricity supplied by Duke Energy. Our desire for affordable power and our desire for environmental protection are often at odds with each other. This is something we really need to consider when we think about bringing electricity to the 1.2.

We need to be frank: there is a true dark side to most forms of electrical generation. We need to acknowledge this before we can make a change. What follows is evidence that shows why we need to find a new way to bring clean, sustainable energy to a billion people around the world, and then use that knowledge to redo the existing grids in high-income nations. When you see the true costs of producing electricity, you can also see the great benefits of finding a new way forward.

SHOCKING

I've read stories of death from electricity all around the world, from India to the UK to the US. The most obvious danger from electricity is that it kills people who fiddle with the wires without having the necessary skills. Theft of electricity is a huge problem around the world, and lots of people are electrocuted while illegally tapping into lines. I've read stories of deaths in Jamaica, Nigeria, England, India, Ohio, and elsewhere. At Duke Energy we investigated thousands of cases of electricity theft, and recovered millions of dollars in stolen fees from "customers,"[2] although I'm not aware of any who died while tapping into our lines.

That just means we were lucky, though. Around the world, it seems like there's no shortage of people willing to risk severe injury or death to get power for free. The potential loss of life is much more alarming than the theft itself. I recently read about a Detroit man who burned to death high up on a utility pole while trying to tap into free power for a squatter's camp.[3]

It's not just humans who are affected by touching live wires. I was surprised, and a little upset, to read that even elephants in India are routinely killed by contact with errant wires. Recently 28 elephants were electrocuted by low-hanging power lines in one Indian state alone. Several hundred may have died elsewhere in India in the last decade due to poorly maintained wires.[4]

Electricity is a force of nature. When we try to manage it, there are all sorts of consequences. It's important to consider how to mitigate the consequences of generating and transmitting power as we bring electricity to those who lack it. We'll start by looking at how we can reduce the damage caused by coal.

THE DIRTY FUEL

Historically, coal has powered nearly half the electrical generation in the United States, and about 75 percent in India and China.[5] In the last decade, new, highly productive methods of extracting natural gas, along with the increased use of renewables, have caused the use of coal to drop to just 39 percent of electrical generation in the US, but this isn't the case in the rest of the world. Even as China explores new sources of energy, the government continues to build coal-fired electric plants at a speedy rate, though perhaps that will slow following the 2014 US-China agreement to reduce greenhouse gas emissions over time. Every kilowatt-hour of electricity produced using coal creates about two pounds of carbon dioxide. That's about a third more than is produced by natural gas. It would be great if we could say that clean energy is poised to solve these problems, but right now solar, hydropower, and wind barely produce any power at all. Even nuclear only makes a tiny contribution. I know, because I used to run all these different kinds of power generators.

When you add in the coal used to make steel, cement, and other products, China burns more coal by itself than all the other countries of the world combined. Which is part of the reason China is responsible for about a quarter of all the greenhouse gases emitted worldwide. China has broadened its efforts to develop clean sources of power, such as wind and solar, but most experts believe that the country's carbon output has not yet peaked.

But it's not just China that's burning coal at an unprecedented rate. Despite scientists, political leaders, and thinkers around the world insisting that we need to scale back our burning of fossil fuels, construction of coal-fired plants continues unabated. The World Resources Institute estimates there are about 1,200 new coal-burning plants being built around the globe, from Europe to Australia (most, but not all are geared toward producing electricity).[6]

That's a lot of coal. All of it comes from out of the ground, and most of it ends up as light, air-conditioning, and other wonderful benefits in our homes and businesses. We love these things, but we hate the pollution that makes them possible. It's easy to blame the utilities, or the greedy capitalists, or other groups, but in truth, each one of us is complicit each time we flip a light switch. It's just a fact.

During my years with electrical utilities, I watched many thousands of coal trains arrive at my plants to fuel the turbines that churned out the electricity we'd send to the far reaches of the country.

These trains are spectacular examples of human ingenuity and determination. In a digital age in which everything important seems to fit on a screen, and nothing seems quite "real," these trains are potent reminders that we're still dependent on the industrial age. Picture a train rising out of a coal depot in the Montana high plains, car after car filled with recently mined lump coal.[7] It's a majestic sight, even if it's one that must come to an end in the coming decades.

Coal is a plentiful resource, and it has always seemed pretty cheap, until you figure in the environmental costs. The world has started doing just that lately, and it is finally waking up to the fact that something's got to change.

While there's a lot of talk these days about so-called clean coal, the term really should be "cleaner" coal. From the digging of the coal to the disposal of the ash produced when the coal is burned, there's nothing clean about it. New technologies may help, but I don't see anything practical and affordable on the horizon.

We've got a long way to go toward making coal a sustainable source of energy in the current environment. And to tell you the truth, I don't think we'll be able to reduce the carbon emissions from coal in a cost-effective way in the next several decades.

DUST AND DESTRUCTION

Once the coal is taken out of the earth, a lot of dust is lost as the coal trains roar along the tracks, wind whipping their cargo. A fine coal dust blankets the countryside, getting into people's lungs. The trains sometimes carry coal as far as from Montana, where there are huge coalfields, to power plants in Georgia on the other side of the continent. And that's just the domestic movement. Ships carry coal across the oceans to fuel coal-fired electrical plants in India and China. Imagine that—a giant ship full of coal crossing the Pacific Ocean. It doesn't seem very practical. But our coal is of a finer quality than much of the coal in China, so there's a market for it.

To make the coal more compact for shipping, it is often crushed and washed to remove impurities and non-coal materials that would just take up unnecessary space on the trains. While this reduces the environmental impact of the train trips themselves, the washing leaves behind huge amounts of toxic residue, often stored in gigantic toxic reservoirs.

The Union of Concerned Scientists estimates that over 700 of these slurry reservoirs, containing hundreds of millions of gallons of mine waste dot America's Appalachian region alone. Sometimes these reservoirs fail. In 2000, a dam failed near Inez, Kentucky, sending over 300 million gallons of so-called "black water" into two creeks that feed the Ohio River. It was an eerie sight: the once pristine creeks of my home state flowing black and tarry through grassy green banks. All told, the volume of slurry leaked was equal to nearly 30 Exxon Valdez spills.[8]

Coal production and burning also require huge amounts of water. Some of that becomes highly polluted and needs to be cleaned, so it won't contaminate rivers. However, we return 98 percent of the water we use for production of electricity back to the rivers, losing 2 percent in the process to evaporation. Various types of coal produce different pollutants, but all have a huge problem with toxic emissions—such as sulfur dioxide, mercury, and tiny particulates—when burned. New plants are built with scrubbers and filter technology that reduce these emissions, and some of the older plants have been retrofitted. I oversaw much of this type of pollution control during my time at Duke Energy, and I'm proud of what we did.

CAPTURING CARBON

What do you do with the waste materials you collect in your attempt to keep them from polluting the environment? There's a lot of talk these days about something called carbon sequestration, whereby the carbon emitted from burning coal would be captured and stored in vast underground storage areas—the same places emptied out by oil and coal removal. The idea is that we'd keep the carbon out of the atmosphere this way. But in truth, it's still an aspirational technology.

Carbon sequestration can be done before the coal is burned, in a process that turns the coal into synthetic gas, which is the cheapest method. Or it can be done after the coal is burned, which is more expensive. Yet both methods are incredibly energy intensive and costly. And because it takes so much energy to extract the carbon, a plant's energy output can easily be reduced by 20 percent. That means you have to burn 20 percent more coal to get the same amount of usable energy, which essentially puts you back at square one.[9]

The first carbon capture and storage (CCS) plant to go online is in Estevan, Saskatchewan, in Canada. It cost over $1 billion to construct, and only treats one of the four generators at the Boundary Dam coal-burning station. Because it reduces the plant's electricity output, the cost to produce power may be higher than the price at which it can be sold. SaskPower, the utility that runs the plant, recovers some of the loss by selling the carbon it captures to oil producers who pump it into their wells to improve production. On the bright side, SaskPower feels it learned so much from building this first plant that it could save $200 million on the cost of constructing the next one.[10]

CHINA IS LEADING THE WAY in developing carbon capture sequestration and integrated gasification combined cycle technologies, but I think the technologies are still a long way from being affordable. And, of course, capturing toxins and storing them is a tricky business. People say that we can store the carbon we sequester underground, but do we really know how stable it will be? One of the challenges I had when operating a gas storage operation decades ago was the migration of gas from underground areas. Storing underground can be problematic. Even storing waste above ground can be a problem. In 2014, a few months after I stepped down as chairman of Duke Energy, we learned that a storage "pond" in which Duke had isolated coal ash, a waste product of coal burning, had leaked into North Carolina's Dan River. This presented very serious issues for the environment, and the company.

While Duke has a plan in place to deal with the issue, it's still symbolic of all that's wrong with coal. And a good reason why we can't stay on this same path forever. Bringing our large-scale industrial electricity production to the 1.2 could be a disaster for their local environments, and the world.

GAS

A technological transformation of America's energy economy started in the first years of this century, and is spreading to China and elsewhere. I'm talking about the highly controversial natural gas extraction technique known as hydraulic fracturing, or fracking, which is used to access deep shale reservoirs of natural gas. Because this method opens up previously out-of-reach stores of natural gas, it has led to a drop in energy prices in the United States along with a rise in manufacturing and—most startling of all—a huge reduction of America's carbon footprint.

Presently, gas is cheaper than coal, which is positive because gas has a fifty percent smaller carbon footprint than coal. The boom in natural gas has actually reduced America's carbon output—a shocking outcome, really, that transpired without government intervention. Energy-related carbon output in the US has dropped by 8.2 percent since 2007. Some think the long recession also helped bring that figure down.[11]

This also means that, as coal and nuclear plants in the US and elsewhere age, the tendency is to replace them with natural gas–powered plants, given the lower cost of using gas. So as gas use increases, it's becoming more important to look at the environmental impacts of extracting and burning gas.[12]

Fracking accounts for 60 percent of all new drilling for natural gas. To use this technology, vertical bore holes are made up to a mile underground,[13] with horizontal shafts branching off to the sides. Frackers inject large amounts of sand, chemicals, and water into the ground at high pressure to break up striated shale rocks far underneath the surface of the earth so that the natural gas flows out more easily. After that, the fracking liquid is pumped out of the ground, allowing the gas to escape and be harvested. Although new practices are being developed to reduce the impact, it has nonetheless been customary to pump the fracking liquid back into the ground for permanent storage.

Theoretically, the fracking liquid is stored far below the water table, which generally goes no deeper than 300 feet. But in truth, no one knows exactly how this waste by-product will behave in the long run, or whether it sometimes creeps up to the surface. In my view, this seems unlikely, but there are plenty of people who say that fracking has ruined their drinking water. We just don't have enough experience with it to know for sure.[14]

I generally support the technique, and I believe the good about fracking outweighs the bad. But I understand how controversial it is, and know that many people are vehemently opposed. New York State has banned fracking, saying it hasn't been proved to be safe. I'm not blind to the suggestion that there are problems associated with fracking that we should look into, but overall, I think it's been good for our country.

IN THE EARLY DAYS of widespread fracking, wells were usually pretty far from people; now holes are being drilled near towns and urban areas, especially in the crowded northeast. This isn't surprising, since the nation's largest shale gas deposit is found in the Marcellus shale, which runs underground on the crowded corridor between New York and Virginia. This could be a problem.

Even I must pause in my praise when I read that the New York State Department of Environmental Conservation has found that fracking companies use over 260 chemicals. Many of these chemicals, like benzene, are highly toxic. Everyone knows that people often make mistakes. What if a producer sends these chemicals into our drinking water? The wastewater from fracking isn't pretty, and no one would want to drink it. And what becomes of the chemicals that are stored underground? Will they have some as yet unknown impact on our lives, or the health of the planet? Even though the Environmental Protection Agency has declared that fracking is basically harmless, the *New York Times* reported the following incidents:

- A poorly drilled well in Bainbridge, Ohio, polluted groundwater for the township police station, and gas from a well migrated through the ground and blew up a house.
- In Dimock, Pennsylvania, near Scranton, 13 water wells were contaminated by natural gas, including one well that exploded and blew up.
- The EPA found traces of methane and a toxic foaming agent in several wells. They didn't trace it directly to the fracking operations happening in the area.
- At least one Pennsylvania homeowner's well was contaminated by fracking, and the company responsible now has to supply her with bottled drinking water. She was paid all of $180 for the rights to drill on her property—many others are far better paid.

Curiously, most state governments do not require fracking companies to disclose what chemicals they use in the extraction process.[15]

Another possible side effect of fracking is perhaps even more alarming: earthquakes. General seismic activity in Oklahoma is now 40 times higher than it was in 2008, say Cornell University scientists.[16]

This seismic increase is vividly illustrated by a look at Jones, Oklahoma, an area better known for the thump of a bull rider hitting the ground than the frightening tremors of a quake. Between 2009 and 2014 there were over 2,500 tiny earthquakes in Jones. In years past, the entire state averaged only about two earthquakes per year. That is a jump of over 1,200 percent. A new study by Cornell University scientists says the increase correlates with an increase in fracking. Specifically, the study finds a correlation between four high-pressure injection wells, where wastewater from fracking is stored, and the increase in earthquakes. The scientists think that the intense pressure used to inject the wastewater deep into the earth lubricates faults, increasing the likelihood of earthquakes.

The researchers support their conclusion with reference to other studies that have found a link between fracking and earthquakes in Arkansas, Ohio, and Texas. They suggest that wastewater from fracking has pushed Oklahoma into the number two spot for earthquakes in the nation, behind California.[17] After years of denying the link, in April 2015 the Oklahoma Geological Survey agreed that the earthquakes in Sooner country are caused by underground storage of wastewater from oil and gas wells.[18] Subsequently, the US Geological Survey identified 17 areas of the US where earthquakes appear to be linked to oil and gas drilling.[19]

PERHAPS MORE SCARY than mild earthquakes in Oklahoma is the possibility that the fracking process is releasing huge amounts of methane into the air. Methane is a by-product of gas production that, over a 100-year period, is 21 times more dangerous for the environment than carbon dioxide, according to the US Environmental Protection Agency. The Intergovernmental Panel on Climate Change, an international organization, estimates that methane gas is 34 times more potent than carbon dioxide. Whichever figure is correct, the risk is huge.

So, while greenhouse gas emissions are down because we're burning more gas than coal, leaking methane from the extraction and transportation of natural gas, which goes largely unacknowledged, offsets some of the gains in terms of climate change.[20] A 2015 Environmental Defense Fund report found that 3.6 trillion cubic feet of methane leaked from oil and gas extraction operations throughout the world each year. That is a huge amount of methane, with an estimated value of $50 billion. If this methane were captured, it would have a large positive effect on climate change.[21] In any event, the US government in 2015 instituted a set of rules meant to govern fracking on federal lands. I hope that these laws help reduce any problems with the technology.

NUCLEAR POWER

Three names sum up most people's fears about nuclear power: Three Mile Island, Chernobyl, and Fukushima. And while each of those reactor meltdowns had its own unique scenario, all three were equally, and understandably, terrifying.

In 1979, one of the two nuclear reactors at Three Mile Island, in Pennsylvania, had a partial meltdown. According to the International Nuclear Event Scale, this meltdown rated 5 out of 7 points. While the accident was caused by mechanical failures, people working at the plant managed to make everything worse. It later came out that some workers weren't well trained and also that the equipment they used wasn't well designed—between the bad design and the workers inexperience, no one could tell from the control room instruments exactly what was happening.

No people died as a consequence of the meltdown, and no radiation was emitted. But the accident upset many people and led to more government regulations and pretty much stalled America's nuclear energy program for decades. Existing plans to build 51 nuclear reactors in the US in the following five years were canceled after the Three Mile Island meltdown.

Cleaning up the mess took 14 years and cost $1 billion. This incredible effort highlighted the incredible unease many people have about nuclear power.

Chernobyl, which melted down in 1986, is a whole different story. The accident, in an area that is now part of the Ukraine, and was then part of the Soviet Union, grew out of a series of occurrences: it started with a power surge that led to a rupture in a reactor, causing a series of steam explosions and a fire, which sent radioactive fallout into the air that spread over a huge area of the Soviet Union and Europe.

Soon after the explosion, firefighters arrived to put out the fires, not knowing the flames were from a nuclear accident. They found themselves trying to extinguish a fire while trying to avoid scattered fragments of radioactive graphite rods from the reactor. Eventually, the fire grew and helicopters were called in to drop sand, lead, clay, and boron into the reactor. One of the helicopters crashed, killing four people. One of the firefighters who battled the flames inside the plant told a reporter that the radiation tasted like metal, and that he felt pins and needles all over his face; he died a short time later.

Despite the magnitude of the problem, the disaster was largely kept secret from the world for two days. The Soviet government didn't admit what had happened until after high radiation levels were detected in Sweden.

A few days after the accident, the state-run TV news explained the situation with this bulletin:

There has been an accident at the Chernobyl Nuclear Power Plant. One of the nuclear reactors was damaged. The effects of the accident are being remedied. Assistance has been provided for any affected people. An investigative commission has been set up.

—*Vremya*, 28 April 1986[22]

Pripyat, the closest city to the disaster, was evacuated. Residents were told to take only what they needed for three days, because they'd soon be returning to their homes. An exclusion zone was established around the area. Three days turned into forever. No one ever returned to collect their things.

Over 230 people suffered acute radiation illness after the Chernobyl disaster. At least 31 died during the accident; another 29 were said to have died in the next few years from radiation exposure. Conservative estimates are that a total of 4,000 will eventually die from their dose of Chernobyl radiation. Among those 4,000 people are some of the estimated 40,000 to 75,000 people who will get cancer because of the accident.

After the accident, the area around Chernobyl suddenly became a ghost town, with hundreds of thousands of inhabitants fleeing for safer locales. Those few who remained soon found themselves in a new world, in which wild animals roamed freely and nature grew untamed, except four square miles of forest that mysteriously turned red and died. Horses and other livestock died. The drinking water for Kiev, a large city in the Ukraine, absorbed high levels of radiation.

In many European countries, where people were exposed to increased radiation levels from the fallout, pregnant women sought abortions out of fear that their fetuses were compromised. The food supply and livestock were closely monitored throughout Europe.

Some farms in the Ukraine reported hundreds of animals born with deformed limbs, missing eyes, and extra extremities in the years following the accident. But the World Health Organization reported that no human deformities were found.

THE ACCIDENT WAS RATED 7 out of 7 on the Nuclear Event Scale. Over half a million people were recruited to clean up the mess, at a cost of over $18 billion (US).

While no one now lives in the area, adventure tourists can make short visits to see what life is like when humans leave and wildlife takes over. They are instructed to stick close to their guides, as there are still radioactive hot spots in Pripyat.

IN 2011, THE FUKUSHIMA nuclear reactor in Japan was damaged by a tsunami triggered by a magnitude 9.0 earthquake off the west coast of Japan. Three of Fukushima's six reactors melted down, leading it to become the second disaster, after Chernobyl, rated a 7 on the Nuclear Event Scale. The accident raised this question: Why was the reactor not better protected given that it was so close to the sea?

No one died in the immediate meltdown, but 600 people were said to have died during the evacuation of the radiation area, on top of the 16,000 who died from the earthquake and tsunami. The resulting contamination was massive, with the Japanese Science Ministry reporting that radioactive cesium contaminated 11,580 square miles of the countryside. A 4,500-square-mile area—about the size of Connecticut—had radiation levels above the Japanese government's allowable level. Some radioactive material was released into the ocean off Fukushima, and fish along that coast are still considered unsafe to eat.[23]

AS WITH CHERNOBYL, there is still a broad exclusion zone around the plant.

One investigation found that the disaster could have been predicted, if anyone had bothered to examine the data and act on it.

The investigation also found that many of the aftereffects, including radioactive water that leaked out of containment areas, could have been prevented. This is perhaps the biggest nightmare for all nuclear facilities—no matter how safe the power generation process *can* be, it will only be as safe as the people who run it.

I give you all these details of the horrors of a nuclear meltdown as a prelude to my belief that nuclear plants are among the safest ways we have to generate electricity. Most important, if you are serious about addressing climate change, you need to be serious about building new nuclear plants. Nuclear energy is the only technology that produces carbon-free electricity 24/7. Approximately 64 percent of the carbon-free electricity in the US comes from nuclear. I hope, actually, that in the future the construction of nuclear plants becomes cheap enough to situate more of them, of all sizes, around the world, to run grids cleanly and efficiently.

No matter how horrible these three accidents were, they are the only three major nuclear accidents that have occurred in over 15,000 combined years of running nuclear reactors, in 33 countries. So the risk of accidents is small, though the consequences, when they do happen, can be huge.

Aside from accidents, however, the biggest challenge we face in the operation of nuclear plants is the storage of spent nuclear fuel. As of right now, we don't really know what to do with spent fuel. There's been a drawn-out process of trying to store it deep inside Yucca Mountain in Nevada. This is a safe location where radioactive elements won't get into the environment and people won't be able to steal it. Yet the US government, after taking $30 billion from US consumers to pay for the idea, has failed to fulfill its obligations to store this spent fuel. Yucca Mountain needs to be opened.

For now, nuclear plants store spent fuel above or below ground in steel-lined concrete vaults filled with water. The yard behind Duke's Catawba Nuclear Energy facility in South Carolina, for instance, has secure above-ground concrete bunkers filled with spent fuel. It's well-guarded, for sure, and I don't think anyone would be able to steal it, or that it would be able to contaminate us in the near future. But future generations will also be dealing with this by-product of "clean" power. And every nuclear plant has stockpiles of spent waste sitting around waiting for a solution. The thought of trying to store something safely for hundreds of thousands of years truly seems absurd, doesn't it? But that's the only option currently being considered in the US when it comes to spent nuclear fuels, even though the French have safely and economically recycled spent fuel rods for more than 40 years.

Nuclear plants often have other, less immediately disastrous effects. As with coal- and gas-fired plants, nuclear plants heat water to create steam that rotates the turbines that make electricity. They also use water as a cooling agent. The water is usually collected from lakes, rivers, or sea inlets, and this can ruin local aquatic habitats. Creatures like fish, manatees, sea turtles, and others, some of which are attracted by the warmer water around nuclear plants, are sometimes sucked into the filters and killed.[24] Still, 98 percent of the water is returned to the source after the cooling process and 2 percent evaporation.

All of these drawbacks are part of the reality of electricity as we use it now. Surely, some of these generating techniques will be refined and improved and used well into the next 100 years. But it's also clear that bringing these giant issues to areas of the world that have no electricity is not the answer. From one perspective, the areas that have not developed complex industrial grids are quite lucky. They can build up their electrical supply using more environmentally sound technologies, with the benefit of knowing what is harmful and what isn't. The declining cost of renewables is making them a more affordable option. They will be able to skip the industrial stage, with its dangers, and jump right into a brave—and clean— new world.

7

THE FUTURE OF POWER

IN MY DECADES AS THE CEO OF VARIOUS ELECTRIC UTIL-
ities, I often saw a schism between people's need for reliable, affordable power and their desire not to harm the environment. As head of
these utilities, I could clearly see that there was always a tradeoff—if
you wanted a lot of electricity, you had to risk polluting the air, water, or forests. But for a long time now I have harbored the hope that,
one day soon, technology would bring about a new and better way of
producing electricity, something we hadn't yet discovered that would
give us vast amounts of affordable electricity, with little or no harm
to the planet.

While we've made a lot of progress toward clean, affordable energy with solar technology, no one's come up with any silver bullets—
though I think we're getting closer. Lately there have been some pretty
interesting developments that might become miracle cures sometime
in the future. Wouldn't it be great if the problem of electricity for the
1.2 could be solved with a brilliant new technological fix? Here are a
few of the innovative ideas that are worth watching.

NEW IDEAS

One interesting new idea takes solar and supersizes it. Existing
solar panels convert only 15 to 20 percent of the energy that hits

them into electricity, because they can only absorb certain light rays coming from the sun. Helped by a \$2.7 million grant from the US Advanced Research Projects Agency for Energy (ARPA-E), scientists at the California Institute of Technology are developing a series of solar cells that absorb different parts of the light spectrum. According to Harry Atwater, a professor at Caltech, when these cells are linked together in a panel, they manage to absorb a higher percentage of the sun's rays. This means that these new modules could convert about 50 percent of the sunlight that hits them—three times the efficiency of traditional modules. So far, no one has developed a practical application for this idea, though it is hoped that the technology might eventually lower both the cost and the footprint of solar energy.

If this or other new technology is able to produce even more solar power, the question will be how to take advantage of that power after the sun goes down, so it isn't wasted. This is actually the entire key to 24/7 solar energy. The energy in coal and gas can be distributed day and night, just by flicking a switch to heat up the steam to spin the turbines. Obviously, the sun sets every day, which leads to the biggest problem with solar and wind power: it stops flowing when the wind dies down or the sun sets. Often, that happens just when the most people need power at home to make dinner, study, and do other tasks after dark. But solar and wind power can also cut out during the daytime—during, say, a rainstorm.

You could solve this problem with the right battery or storage device. In effect, if you could combine battery storage with wind and solar energy, you could make fuel that was basically free. That's a huge possibility, the consequences of which are almost too big to imagine.[1]

RESERVOIR OF ELECTRICITY

As of now, there are still no affordable and viable options for storing electricity on a large scale, except for a few that only work in very specific situations. That means that solar and wind power can't be the basis for commercial grids, in most cases, because grids need a predictable output of power, 24 hours a day, 7 days a week.

One of the oldest systems for storing electricity is called pumped hydroelectric power. First used in the late nineteenth century in Europe, this system relies on two water reservoirs, one high up and one lower down, and turbines, to provide a steady source of power. This is a great method for supplying power to a remote area, if the terrain can support it.

In my career I've operated two pumped hydrostorage plants that were among the largest in the US. One was called Bad Creek pump hydrostorage plant, and the other was Jocassee pump hydrostorage plant. Both were located in South Carolina. Combined they had 1,775 megawatts, which is a lot of power. These days, hydrostorage is an expensive proposition in the US, but there are interesting projects being developed in other parts of the world.

A surprising modern example of pumped hydroelectric power is found on the island of El Hierro, the smallest inhabited island in Spain's Canary Islands archipelago, and perhaps the only island in the world to, in effect, have turned itself into a giant battery.

With steep cliffs that face the strong winds blowing off the Atlantic coast of northwest Africa, the island has plenty of exposure to the wind's energy. Recently, the island's 10,000 residents began relying on a five-turbine wind farm for power. To ensure there is enough power even when the wind isn't blowing, El Hierro uses two large reservoirs, one built at the top of a cliff in the crater of an old volcano and the other at the bottom of the cliff. When a strong wind is blowing, and there's plenty of power, some of that excess electricity is used to pump water from the lower reservoir to the upper reservoir. Then, when the wind dies down, or demand peaks, water can be released from the upper reservoir to fall down through turbines at the lower reservoir, creating additional power. It's a simple and elegant system that was designed to pay for itself, with minimal environmental impact. Perfect for El Hierro and other locales that have cliffs, wind, and empty space for reservoirs.[2]

BATTERIES

Batteries, of course, are a more common option for storing solar and wind energy, and there have been some promising recent discoveries on the battery front. Most batteries—from clunky old lead batteries to sleek new lithium-ion batteries—are made from two types of electrodes and an electrolyte that lets ions move between the electrodes, allowing for usable current.

During the last years of my time at Duke Energy we pilot tested seven different kinds and sizes of battery technologies on our grid.

We put some in substations and others in power plants and other key locations throughout the grid, and Duke Energy is continuing to explore ways to use battery technology to improve the resilience of the grid. I believe that grid-level storage will transform the operation of the grid when it becomes more affordable. And lessons learned from developing this storage technology will be applicable in microgrids in the low-income world.

A promising innovation came about when inventors tweaked these materials to make them work better. In traditional batteries, the electrical charge is held in the electrodes, but new "flow" batteries store the charge in the electrolyte medium itself, making it possible to build significantly larger batteries that have the potential to be useful for storing wind- and solar-generated energy.[3]

For many years lithium batteries were not economically or technically feasible. Recently they have undergone a revolution in design. New lithium batteries that use silicone wires barely one-thousandth as thick as a sheet of paper have improved lithium storage capacity tenfold. While these batteries are now too expensive for most applications in low-income countries, the price will surely come down soon, and the batteries show great promise for rural power supplies. For perspective, just remember what flat-screen TVs cost when they were first introduced, compared to the price now. Technology generally gets (much) cheaper as it is adopted.

Nanotechnology is probably the future of battery storage. An Ohio company called Nanotek Instruments is leading the way in the development of high-capacity, fast battery systems using a material called graphene. This material, which remains somewhat mysterious to me, lets batteries charge and discharge rapidly tens of thousands of times before degrading to the point where they can't store power well—that's far more recharges than with traditional batteries.

Of course, the high-tech solutions are fantastic, but sometimes what most intrigues me are the simplest, lowest-cost options, such as one proposed by the IBM Research Lab in Bangalore, India. According to researchers at the lab, millions of laptop batteries that are discarded each year still have enough rechargeable nature left to power a solar home lighting system. In fact, 70 percent of the discarded batteries they tested were good enough to power an LED light four hours a day for a year. Since batteries are often the most expensive part of home solar systems, this news could save a lot of money while helping to light the world.

NO TREES, LOTS OF ENERGY

During my time at Duke Energy we started a division called Duke Energy Renewables, as part our commercial businesses arm. The idea was to develop innovative wind and solar energy projects that could help utilities deliver reliable and relatively clean energy to their customers, as a necessary step in reducing carbon emissions and mitigating the effects of climate change.

Under my watch, Duke invested $4 billion in wind and solar power and in advanced technologies such as the novel Notrees Battery Storage Project.[4] Notrees is an area of West Texas that got its name from its lack of trees—supposedly, its single native tree was cut down in the mid-twentieth century to make room for a gas plant.[5] The winds in Notrees are strong and steady, and on my first visit to the area I feared I was going to be blown over. The locals, partial to Texas hyperbole, say the winds are so strong that the only thing that separates the panhandle of Texas from the North Pole are the barbed wire fences.

Given the winds, Notrees seemed like a good place for Duke Energy to invest in a large wind power operation. In 2009, once the wind farm was in place, Duke Energy matched a $22 million grant from the US Department of Energy to install large-scale batteries to store power from the 153-megawatt wind farm at Notrees. The 36-megawatt battery, known as a dynamic power resource, was designed and installed by Xtreme Power of Austin, Texas. Without battery storage, wind and solar power just won't be effective in the long term. While not perfect, this project demonstrates how well battery storage enhances wind power, by backing up electricity when the wind is down, and the need is high. It also helps to stabilize the flow of power through the grid.

All in all, the project was a huge success.

"Completion of this project represents a singular success for Duke Energy, for the DOE, and for the entire energy storage community in the US." said Dr. Imre Gyuk, program manager for energy storage at the US Department of Energy. "It will demonstrate the capability of energy storage to mitigate the variability of wind energy and to contribute to the stability of the grid."[6]

Without a doubt, improved battery technology will be a good thing for low-income countries as they expand further into renewables like solar and wind. These giant batteries will be key to making mini-grids, and even larger alternative power grids, function well.

Batteries are also a good option for home storage systems. Right now, many households around the globe harvest energy from sunlight during the day and store it in various types of batteries, from traditional car batteries to lithium-ion batteries used to power not only computers, but even electric cars, such as those made by Tesla.

The newer generation of lithium batteries are 30 to 40 percent more efficient than the older versions; that efficiency will surely improve rapidly, making the batteries even more useful for home solar systems.[7] But all these batteries, especially the more old-fashioned car batteries, have to be maintained, and that can be an issue in rural areas, as I discussed in chapter 4.

HYDROGEN HOPES

Other, more exotic uses for maximizing the potential solar power are also being explored. Chemical storage solutions, such as hydrogen, are very interesting because they are cleaner than any of the alternatives. If you charge a hydrogen system with solar or wind power, there are virtually zero emissions. The technology, while promising, needs more research. But there's a lot of intriguing stuff happening.

For instance, a group of Swiss, Korean, and Singaporean scientists say they've figured out a better way to convert solar energy into hydrogen power. Since hydrogen can be easily stored, and easily used as fuel, this could solve the ongoing problem of how to store sunlight's energy for use after dark.

The scientists built something called a "water splitter"—a device that's more efficient at turning solar power into hydrogen than any other before it. It uses surplus energy to split water into hydrogen and oxygen; the hydrogen is then turned into methane that is burned to make electricity. It's a relatively inexpensive, efficient, and reliable process, and uses only widely available materials.

According to Michael Graetzel, director of the Laboratory of Photonics and Interfaces at the École Polytechnique, in Switzerland, the group's research builds on work they and other scientists have been doing for decades. The difference now is that the water-splitter equipment depends on high-output solar panels built with a novel photovoltaic material called perovskite. The use of perovskite, together with the solar splitter, allows scientists to store a little over 12 percent of the energy in sunlight as hydrogen. While a traditional solar panel converts approximately 16 percent of the energy of sunlight into electricity, that energy must then be stored or distributed immediately, at a loss of efficiency. If the water splitter proves successful, this new method would enable the energy to be used at a later time—thus functioning just like a battery.

The water splitter isn't yet practical for the marketplace, but scientists hope a commercial system will be up and running soon.[8] I consider this an important technology to watch, especially as a method for those people who are moving up the electricity ladder from simple lighting to more complex systems.

SPEAKING OF HYDROGEN, this fuel has long been hailed as our best hope for saving the environment. I'm skeptical because this has been touted for some time, but is still very far from being ready for the market. Nonetheless there is some interesting work going on with hydrogen fuel cells. It's possible that this technology will come down in price enough to be affordable, and widely used in rural areas of the low-income world.

These fuel cells use a combination of hydrogen and oxygen to initiate a chemical reaction that makes electricity. For several decades they've been the "next big thing," because people hope that there will be an abundant source of pollution-free fuel. The only byproduct of hydrogen fuel cells is water. However, hydrogen fuel has to be harvested from somewhere—in the US it generally comes from natural gas, but it can also come from coal or biomass. So, carbon is generally involved in producing this clean fuel, unless the hydrogen fuel is harvested using emissions-free (not counting nuclear waste that must be stored) nuclear power to send electricity into water to separate the hydrogen and oxygen.

Fuel cells are being used right now. For example, Walmart has committed to using hydrogen fuel cells to power over 1,700 forklifts in the US,[9] power plants based on fuel cells are powering some neighborhoods in Korean cities, and hydrogen fuel cells are helping to power data centers and office parks in various parts of the world. If the technology does become broadly practical—a big if, from my perspective, due to the very high cost and also some serious safety issues—fuel cells could be very helpful in bringing large amounts of clean power to people in remote areas of the earth.

ENERGIES OF INVENTION

From Silicon Valley tech entrepreneurs to Detroit urban farmers, our culture is exploding with innovative thinking right now, and nowhere more so than in energy research. An example of this innovation is the shiny winged donut designed to hover in the sky above Anchorage, Alaska. A company called Altaeros Energies has designed a floating wind generator it calls the Buoyant Airborne Turbine (BAT) that is shaped like a large donut. It is meant to float in the steady wind currents a few hundred feet off the ground. A turbine spins in the "donut hole," sending electricity to the ground via a cable. The device is designed to replace diesel generators, especially in places energy is needed quickly, such as after a disaster. But the donut could also be used in remote places that need power.[10]

Several other companies are also doing interesting work with airborne generators. Makani Power, now owned by Google, is working on a fixed wing "kite," with several turbines. It flies at an altitude of about 1,000 feet, where the wind is strong enough to spin the turbines at 250 miles per hour. The electricity generated is sent to the ground via tethers. Other companies exploring the airborne turbine route include WindLift, SkySails, Sky Windpower, and NTS. Ben Franklin would have loved it.

Despite all the technological and regulatory obstacles these companies face, I believe they show tremendous potential. The floating turbines are fanciful and surprising, and should prove to be less expensive than the giant fixed wind turbines that now dot the landscape around the world. Plus, floating turbines can be installed far out to sea, in deeper water than will support conventional wind turbines, and also in more forbidding terrain on land.[11]

FIRE AND ICE

Methane hydrate, or crystalline natural gas, is another potential source of energy that could change the whole equation of electrical distribution. This surprising gas wasn't even discovered until the 1970s, probably because it lies encased in striated layers of ice at the bottom of lakes and oceans, which is why it is called "the ice you can set on fire." It's thought there is more energy in the world's methane hydrate than in all the earth's fossil fuels combined. You might call it the shale gas of the sea.

Only recently have people begun to crack the code of getting this stuff to market. The Japanese are using a half-billion-dollar research ship to harvest methane hydrate off their coast. They are especially interested in this resource, since Japan owns no oil deposits and imports nearly all its energy. Rwanda, a country where fewer than 1 in 10 people has access to electricity, is also moving into the methane hydrate arena. The government and private enterprises alike are trying to solve the puzzle of how best to harvest methane hydrate from the bottom of Lake Kivu, a vast, picturesque lake that separates Rwanda from the Congo.

These enterprises have to proceed with great caution, because there are many risks involved with harvesting methane hydrate— explosion is one, the release of huge amounts of carbon into the atmosphere is another. But if they succeed, the technology could change the face of countries like Rwanda. With a ready supply of gas, the government could supply all its citizens with electricity. However, I don't find this to be a great hope for electrifying the 1.2, because when you burn methane hydrate, you increase the effects of climate change. And if there's an endless supply of cheap gas, who is going to bother with solar and wind?[12]

These days, many researchers, including some from Stanford University and Citigroup, believe renewable energy will be price-competitive with fossil fuels in most of the world by 2020. That might chill people's interest in spending tons of money on further developing methane hydrate. Sun and wind, after all, are the most easily distributed, easily harvested energies in the world—for now, at least.

NEW NUCLEAR

Transatomic Power is a very interesting company. Started by two young MIT graduates, it just might have gone a long way toward solving the problem of nuclear waste, and making reactors more safe.

Transatomic claims to have figured out a way to repurpose highly radioactive spent fuel and use it to generate huge amounts of electricity in a method called transnuclear. Right now, nuclear plants use only about 3 percent of the energy in the fuel rods that power nuclear generators. Transatomic's technology will let them access about 96 percent of the available energy, according to computer modeling.[13]

"Right now there are 270,000 tons of spent nuclear fuel in storage," said Leslie Dewan, PhD, cofounder and CEO of Transatomic, at a Solve for X conference.[14] "We could take that waste and with our technology make enough electricity to power the entire world for 70 years. At the same time, we'd get rid of almost all nuclear waste."

The waste generated by a plant running on transnuclear technology would have a shelf life of only hundreds of years, rather than hundreds of thousands. This seems almost like a miracle to me.[15]

Bill Gates and a team of visionaries are working on another nuclear technology called Traveling Wave reactors. These are also powered by the "spent fuel" that traditional reactors store in their backyards.[16]

There's a lot of promise in both of these projects. It will take a long time to implement them, given costs, engineering problems, and government regulations. But this idea of nuclear power has great potential for the low-income world, especially for those people in densely populated areas who now live without electricity. Any large-scale electricity generation, such as nuclear, is harder to distribute to rural areas that have no power lines or other infrastructure.[17]

SEA POWER

Another area for potential power that, like nuclear power, faces problems of distribution in low-income countries, is power generated by the energy of ocean movements. Several interesting projects are now investigating how to harness the seemingly inexhaustible power of ocean tides and currents.[18]

Tidal energy is closer to becoming a commercially viable technology than is harnessing the energy from ocean currents. Tides are more predictable and stable than currents, and thus in some ways are easier to work with. But the ocean presents all sorts of problems, ranging from weather to the corrosive effects of salt water.

Some of the tidal power concepts include the Pelamis P2, which looks a bit like a bright red sea monster. It floats in the sea, converting wave power into electricity, which is sent ashore over underwater lines. Aquamarine power uses a similar concept. Another company, called Ocean Power Technologies, builds buoys that float on the waves, converting wave energy into electricity.[19]

There is much promising research going on in this area; I think it's a potentially viable way to produce very clean electricity. But this brings up the problem of distribution. There are no waves in the interiors of countries, and wave technology would often depend on transmission lines.

That's why my thoughts always return to solar power. It's so simple in many ways. For that reason I really appreciate a new device from Eco Nation that doesn't so much reflect a radical restructuring of technology as it does common sense. Called the LightCatcher, this is an innovative system that uses mirrors and natural sunlight to bring lots of clean, beautiful light to the interiors of dark buildings. At the same time, it helps regulate the heat in a building.

The LightCatcher has mirrors mounted inside a box with a high-tech light dome programmed to search the sky for optimum light. This can be the sun's light, or some other light source if the sun isn't visible. The mirror grabs the light and filters and amplifies it before sending it inside a building to light up the space. This is a great idea. But of course, it only works when the sun or another light source is bright.

The bottom line is that the options for the rural poor today are solar, wind, and biomass (via waste). Other innovations, such as fuel cells and methane hydrate, are on the horizon but may never have practical applications for the 1.2.

8

THE COMING MICROGRIDS

HAVING OVERSEEN MASSIVE AND COMPLEX ELECTRICAL grids serving millions of homes and businesses, I have to admit that the idea of a microgrid is pretty attractive. I mean, the big grids I managed, with their nuclear plants, coal generating stations, dams, and gas plants could be a hell of a headache at times. *Microgrid.* Just saying it lowers my blood pressure a little bit. It sounds so manageable, so easy, almost magical.

By microgrid, I mean locally produced energy that is distributed to homes and businesses nearby—as opposed to a traditional grid, in which the source of the electricity, such as a coal-fired power plant, might be hundreds of miles from home.

In an American city, where the grid penetrates to every street, a microgrid might be a small power plant—solar, fuel cell, or diesel—that keeps electricity flowing into an entire building or complex—like a jail or hospital—that can't afford any disruption in power.

In a rural Indian village, a microgrid might be one central plant that powers a few dozen homes and businesses. The basic microgrid setup in the low-income world is a solar home system consisting of a battery, a power-generating source—such as solar—a few LED lights, and a phone charger. The next step up would be a microgrid that powered several neighboring homes off one power-generating source. Hybrid microgrids are more complex, often using computers to intelligently switch between several different sources of power, like solar and diesel, to make sure service is consistent under all weather conditions and at all levels of demand.

Microgrids are beautiful in several ways. Since they are autonomous, isolated villages can be wired more cheaply with microgrids than by running transmission lines many miles from a power plant. Microgrids aren't subject to the whims of the grids, such as power surges and outages. And microgrids can easily scale up to offer much higher levels of power than the more ubiquitous small solar home systems run by single panels. Microgrids make it easier to power TVs, refrigerators, and computers using clean energy, especially if the appliances are modern and highly energy efficient.[1]

IN MY TIME WORKING with electrical utilities I've seen the science of microgrids advance rapidly. Traditionally, they were powered by noisy, dirty, and expensive diesel generators, but now they increasingly run on all manner of fuels, such as solar, wind, biomass, and gas (often with an old-fashioned diesel generator as a backup). Microgrids are usually designed to fit well with a village's particular environment. In Nepal, for example, there are very successful hydropower microgrids taking advantage of powerful streams and rivers at high altitudes. As of 2013, there were nearly 4,000 megawatts of global microgrid energy, according to the Institute of Electrical and Electronic Engineers.[2]

VARIABLES

Hybrid microgrids, which combine the benefits of various sources of power to make a steadier supply for a community, will work even better.

Microgrids can have a huge effect on people's lives, often much greater than simple solar home systems. The World Bank estimates that the presence of microgrids in a community increases household income by 11 percent over time. But there's a price.

Microgrids are expensive to install and maintain; systems generally cost between $10,000 and $100,000 to install. There's also the matter of maintenance, and the cost of replacing batteries or other storage systems when they fail or wear out. A dysfunctional community will not be able to sustain a microgrid, because there must be a payment and maintenance plan in place that does not wholly depend on outside agencies. For a microgrid to be successful, members of the community must pay for the electricity and oversee much of the day-to-day maintenance themselves.

Population density is another variable in the success of microgrids. Low-density, widely spaced communities will have a harder time supporting a microgrid, and would likely benefit more from home solar systems.[3] Something as basic as proper installation also affects the success of microgrids, so they must be installed by someone who is knowledgeable about community building, the varied needs of villages, and technology and maintenance. Existing utilities, whether in low-income countries or in the West, aren't always the best stewards of these new grids. But sometimes governments choose unschooled utilities to install microgrids in rural areas anyway; often, these efforts fail for a lack of expertise and a lack of incentive.[4]

Many people value microgrids as, at best, a backup to the existing traditional grid. The microgrid can generate energy for the larger grid, and also fill in during power outages. This makes sense in high-income countries, but it's a nonstarter in most of Sub-Saharan Africa, which has almost no grid structure, and also in much of India and Indonesia. Many villages in India are served by a traditional grid that only carries electricity a few hours a day, usually during daylight hours. Microgrids could be joined to these inefficient traditional grids, but I don't think that's the way to go. Far better to start fresh, creating a new system that will leapfrog traditional industrial grids and take us into the future.

A GOOD SYSTEM

I believe this rosy future is still pretty far in the distance. Even though there are some impressive microgrids out there, only a small number are already transforming the lives of rural people who have no other access to electricity. But there are some bright spots. An innovative company called Powerhive is doing impressive work with microgrids in Kenya. Working with First Solar, an American company, Powerhive tested its new metering and control platform in Kisii Province, where 9 out of 10 people lack power. It has an immediate goal of deploying this system to deliver power to 200,000 Kenyan households. The company's data-driven, cloud-based monitoring and mobile telephone payment system lets customers buy their power in advance. I think this demand-driven way of looking at supplying energy is the future of power, not only in low-income countries, but all over the world. I've got a lot of faith in the vision of Christopher

Hornor, Powerhive's president and CEO, and I think the company's technology makes that demand-driven outcome easier.[5]

Some of the most well-known and successful microgrids in the low-income world are those installed in three villages in the Kinabatangan District of Sabah, Malaysia by an Australian company called Optimal Power Solutions. The installation in one of the villages was written up in a widely circulated article in *The MIT Technology Review*,[6] and has become the benchmark for other microgrids. The article described how these villages are so remote that at certain times of the year they are only accessible by boat. The area is a sensitive environment for wild animals, and is one of the last forested floodplains in Asia. All this makes importing diesel very expensive.

The company designed hybrid solar systems to fit the specific needs of the villages, such as their density, population, and power needs. These particular microgrids are backed up by diesel. Since the communities were dependent on diesel generators before the microgrids were built, the new system will reduce diesel use by at least 50 percent, which should help cover the cost of the installations.

The microgrids installed by Optimal Power Solutions are simple and effective, and surprisingly tech-forward. Each grid has a shed that serves as a control center, with computers to manage power for a few hundred people. Using sophisticated software, the computers regulate the power coming in from the solar panels and generators, sending some power out to homes and storing some in large batteries for later use. The computer also notifies a central station when the microgrid is having trouble. Thanks to sophisticated batteries, people in the villages served by OPS now have power 24/7—a remarkable feat that has dramatically changed village life.

A walk through these remote villages today reveals satellite dishes on people's roofs that feed power to flat-screen TVs in their family rooms. Some villagers have rice cookers and other devices. Stores sell refrigerated items. The electricity allows people to work harder, sell more, and earn more. In turn, that lets them buy more. It's a virtuous cycle that wouldn't be possible without the sustainable microgrid. However, the future is yet uncertain. Would the villagers cooperate, paying for the equipment and maintaining it, if Optimal Power Solutions turned total control over to them?

COST GETS IN THE WAY

The cost of microgrids certainly looks attractive when compared to the cost of traditional grids. The government of Malaysia estimates that running a power line 130 kilometers to bring electricity to a village costs about $80 million, which is a pretty high price to pay for supplying electricity to a few hundred people. Malaysia plans to emphasize microgrids, rather than industrial grids, to achieve its goal of bringing electricity to 95 percent of Malaysian Borneo by 2016, up from only 25 percent in 2013.

Even though the International Energy Agency says microgrids are the best way to bring power to communities, I don't always agree. Sure, they work in relatively wealthy countries such as Malaysia, where the government can make a decision to focus on microgrids. But residents of Indian states such as Uttar Pradesh, or a country such as Kenya, can't afford to spend millions on microgrids. Instead, the poorest countries are more likely to focus on the less expensive solar home systems. These systems are fantastic and change lives— but not as much as microgrids. Which approach is a better fit for the average community? It's a question of time and money.

Anyone who has traveled in the rural area of a low-income nation will notice how ubiquitous mobile phones are these days. You can be standing with a Patagonian shepherd in Argentina, hundreds of miles from the nearest large city, and he'll pull out his phone to check on a delivery of supplies to the ranch. In much of the world, people have mobile phones even when they don't have toilets or electricity.

I'm astounded to discover that some low-income nations now have more mobile phone users than do high-income countries. They've completely skipped the analog age. And I believe the same sudden change will prove true with electrical power. The rural areas of many countries will jump from having no electricity whatsoever to being powered by the latest, most sophisticated solar, wind, and hydropower. Not to mention the potential of less-tested technologies, such as fuel cells. We are at the tipping point of a revolution. Many people believe microgrids will be the defining idea. Navigant Research has predicted that microgrids will provide 1.1 gigawatts of power by 2017, up from just 349 megawatts in 2011. According to Navigant, these remote microgrids will bring in yearly revenues of $8.4 billion by 2020.[7]

MICROGRIDS ARE THE FUTURE

In the past, most microgrids were designed for specialized locations, such as isolated military bases, mining operations, islands, and, sometimes, remote villages. Often these microgrids were powered by diesel that had to be trucked or carried in. The diesel generators blew a lot of pollutants into the air. These days, more and more microgrids are hybrids, using renewable resources backed up by diesel or other fuels. As lithium batteries and other storage options like flywheels improve in the coming years, so will the performance of microgrids. According to the research done by Navigant, sales of energy storage equipment for microgrids (in both low-income and high-income areas) will grow from $662 million in 2014 to $4 billion by 2024. Microgrids definitely improve at the same rate as technology. I predict that in the next three decades microgrids will become the dominant grids around the world.

But, right now, microgrids are not quite ready to provide clean, sustainable energy for the 1.2. They just cost too much.

VILLAGE LIFE

With microgrids, as with other technologies, no matter how good the infrastructure is, it's nothing without reliable maintenance.

Right now, a few hundred villages in India get power from microgrids. One of India's microgrid providers is Mera Gao Power, a company founded by three young men who hope to make kerosene obsolete in India. Working in the province of Uttar Pradesh, they've installed microgrids in a number of villages with some success. These villages generally have brick homes built along narrow lanes, rice fields crisscrossed by dikes, and flowering reeds along lake shores. The countryside is very pretty, but the residents are quite poor by American standards. An electric light is a much-desired luxury here.

Mera Gao defines microgrid as energy that is produced and distributed locally. The word "distributed" is the key difference between a simple solar panel and lights for one house, and a microgrid. Mera Gao might use one larger solar panel, perhaps three feet by four feet, and distribute the resulting electricity to ten houses, with backup energy stored in batteries kept in a little wooden cabinet. The cost of the small microgrid would be $1,000 with a payback period of 2.5 years. That provides each house with two LED lights and a mobile phone charging station. Mera Gao offers full-time support, from local employees, for the systems it installs. The installation is simple: four installers can get one up and running in one day. The company says its systems are completely self-running, able to generate, store, and distribute power without extensive on-site monitoring. The equipment even turns itself off every night to save resources. In 2014 Mera Gao installed equipment for 16,000 households; their goal for 2016 is to reach 50,000 households.

Mera Gao's work was largely financed by a $300,000 grant from the USAID Development Innovation Ventures division.

Another Indian company, Husk Power, has an interesting approach to biomass-generated electricity. The company burns the husks left over from processing the rice that's harvested from ubiquitous fields around the Indian countryside. Among Husk Power's largest projects is a 32-kilowatt system that powers 500 to 700 homes.[8]

While investors hesitate to put money into microgrid projects, because their long-term viability has not yet been proven in many cases, companies are still finding ways to raise capital from both government and private sources. I think the money that is now flowing into microgrids, limited as it is, is a clear indicator of how important the grids are to our future.

INDIA LEADS THE WAY

Recently, India has become very serious about microgrids. The government has decided to boost the country's solar power output target from 20 gigawatts to 100 gigawatts. To put that in perspective, it's about the same amount of power you could get from about 40 midrange coal-burning plants. That's a lot of juice. But how much of that will go to urban and industrial markets, and how much will be targeted for the rural poor, remains to be seen.

With President Obama promoting renewable energy technologies on his 2014 visit to India, there's been talk of lowering trade barriers for clean energy companies. As in much of the world, regulations in India can either help or hurt renewables and microgrids—it's a choice all governments make.[9]

PAYMENT INNOVATIONS

SharedSolar, a company that grew out of work at Columbia University's Earth Institute in New York, has installed scalable microgrids in villages in Africa, such as Ruhiira in Uganda. Here, a small shed houses the electrical equipment, and a few solar panels on the roof collect the sun's energy. The power is distributed over microgrid lines to more than 75 homes and businesses. Customers pay for power in advance, either by purchasing scratch-off cards that contain codes that they can text to SharedSolar via their cell phones, or by going into kiosks that have computer tablets that can do the same thing. Barbers, tailors, and others use the power to work longer hours and make more money.[10] SharedSolar has also installed smaller-scale microgrids in Mali, based on the same system, that power 10 to 20 households.

A VILLAGE CALLED DHARNAI, in Bihar, India, has partnered with the environmental organization Greenpeace on an interesting microgrid project. Now, I've been scolded by Greenpeace in the past for not doing enough to reduce carbon pollution—they even took a full page ad out in the *Charlotte Observer* to knock me down a notch—but I still admire what they've done in Dharnai. The village had government-supplied grid electric back in the twentieth century, but that infrastructure eventually failed, and electricity has been based on diesel generators ever since. Then, along comes Greenpeace to install a 100-kilowatt solar-powered microgrid, which is large enough to power the village's homes and businesses. The switch was turned on in July 2014, by an 80-year-old resident of the village.

The scale of this installation is impressive. It serves about 2,400 people, in about 450 homes. It also powers several dozen businesses, a bunch of streetlights and water pumps, schools, and other services. Just imagine: light for studying, clean water pumped up for drinking, and streetlights for getting around at night. It seems like a minor miracle, but in fact it's just good sense, and creative thinking.

Greenpeace says 80,000 more villages in India could use a solar-powered system like this. Let's make sure they get it.

SWARM THINKING

Then there's a novel idea, proposed by Sebastian Groh, the project manager of MicroEnergy International, called "swarm electrification." It suggests linking together houses that already have their own solar home system, so that a group might share electricity among themselves. This builds off the concept of "swarm intelligence," whereby disparate organisms build off of each other to form a larger intelligence. So the group is greater than the sum of its parts. Power could flow here and there as needed, with no expensive microgrid required.[11]

Ideas like this make me excited for the future. There are so many innovative thinkers out there right now. However, any system, no matter how high-tech and forward-thinking, will require the community's help to succeed. The people being served must be involved, both with payments and with maintenance. This is something to think about when talking about scaling up to provide power to millions of people.

A good microgrid system needs input from those who will use it. The residents of a village know their terrain and their weather, and they know what kinds of organizations will work well in the village. Since the residents may have little experience with electricity, they might not know to what extent they could use it, but they certainly know what to do with the power once it arrives. And they know who has money and how much, and what the community can afford. The residents also know about issues of ethnic, religious, and political tensions that should be considered. All these factors are essential to designing a good microgrid that will last.

Outsiders face a lot of problems when they try to impose a top-down plan designed in a faraway city. When done properly, a microgrid should endure for a couple of decades. When done poorly, the system goes south really quickly. Solar panels aren't cleaned. The jungle grows up fast, blocking the light. Diesel, once the "backup," is used to fill in more and more. The control room becomes a fetid chamber. Finally, the electricity fails and soon the village is back where it started: without power, and without much hope of getting a new system anytime soon. Still, microgrids may be our best hope.

THE LIGHTS STAYED ON

Although I've been at the heart of the traditional energy business for several decades, I'll be the first to admit that our grid system here in the US is in need of significant investment to convert it from an analog grid to a digital grid. I think this transition is critical if we are serious about moving into renewables, large-capacity storage, and optimizing productivity gains by using devices that communicate with each other. Of course microgrids will play a central role in the new electrical landscape.

This was well illustrated when the lights really went out in India in 2012, after three electricity grids tanked, leaving over 600 million people in 20 states around the country without power. From afar, it was easy to see this as a problem of a poorly run grid in a country with a lot of economic and social challenges. However, I didn't see it that way at all. I saw it as a clear example of what was to come for the rest of us. And a challenge to use our imaginations and our human will to get things done. India is not hampered by a dysfunctional grid. Rather, it, like most countries, is hampered by a bureaucracy that slows progress, entrenched carbon energy interests that don't see the benefit of technological change, endemic poverty, and a lack of open markets.

The microgrids installed by Gram Power in the village of Khareda Lakshmipura, in the Indian state of Rajasthan, proved this. During the 2012 blackout, Gram Power's solar-powered microgrid kept homes well lit and small businesses working. This, in a village that is definitely off the grid: To reach Khareda during the rainy season you sometimes have to cross a river in a boat pulled by a man. Yet this small, remote village had fans, TVs, and blenders working as usual when the surrounding countryside was totally in the dark. The power came from a series of solar panels that fed into inverters that could store the power after dark. The power was distributed throughout the village, and a prepaid meter on each home let families monitor their usage and remaining prepayment. The data regarding power and usage was transmitted back to the headquarters of Gram Power in Jaipur.

Think how great it would have been to have systems like this in place when Hurricane Sandy knocked out power to over 8 million homes in the eastern US in 2012. This technology could change the world.

Some private companies, like the software developer Infosys, in India, use microgrids to ensure safe, reliable power for their offices and plants. These aren't clean and sustainable—they depend on fossil fuels, with some added solar power—but they are an important step toward revamping the grid for the future. It's very possible that these microgrids are the harbingers of a network of interconnected, yet separate, power sources.

THE IMPORTANCE OF EFFICIENCY

And now, with hyper-efficient appliances and the Internet of Things, whereby devices can communicate with each other via wireless Internet, embedded systems, and micro-electrical mechanical systems, or MEMS, we're poised to make the power from microgrids (and solar home systems) even more useful. Technology is showing us that it's not just how much power is made, but also how much is used that determines how much electricity a family can have.

For nearly a century, we've created bigger and better appliances, with little thought—until recently—about how much we waste. But it turns out that we can build televisions, refrigerators, air conditioners, and other devices that work well using far less power than previously.

The Super-efficient Equipment and Appliance Deployment, or SEAD, is a joint American-Indian effort to recognize and encourage research into efficient appliances. So far their competitions have recognized televisions that are up to 44 percent more efficient than standard models; computer displays by Samsung and LG that are

28 to 43 percent more efficient, and other highly efficient appliances and lights.

The rapid development of the Internet of Things promises even greater efficiencies. The simplest practical applications for this in everyday life right now are home security systems and thermostats such as the Nest device, which can be controlled remotely via smartphone. But the technology is expanding rapidly; inexpensive, effective tools are coming into the market all the time. The ability of appliances to communicate will help smart microgrids sense power needs before they happen, and also help devices control themselves, so that they use less power.

All these aspects together—smart microgrids, efficient appliances, and innovative and committed customers and installers—give me a lot of hope for the future.

9

ATTRACTING CAPITAL

ALL THE GOOD WISHES IN THE WORLD WON'T BE ENOUGH to bring light to the 1.2 unless there's money backing them up. That's just a fact of modern life. Some ideas require less funding, while others demand a great deal. This one is especially hungry for investment.

Bunker Roy, founder of Barefoot College, believes that he could light the entire world sufficiently for under $100 million. He says way too much money is wasted on overly complex technology, infrastructure, and administration in current top-down efforts to spread solar to rural areas around the globe. Knowing Roy, I wouldn't put it past him to pull off a miracle like this, and I hope he takes on this task, but I think he may be underestimating the cost. The International Energy Association says we'll need to spend $756 billion total, or $36 billion annually, to provide universal access to electricity by 2030, with much of that new power coming from renewable energy. That might sound like a staggering figure but it's not much compared to the amount of capital deployed in high-income countries annually, which is easily hundreds of billions. I'm certain the return on the investment will be well worth it—both the financial return for social enterprises and others that do the work, and the societal returns that come from bettering the lives of over one billion people. When bankers at places like Goldman Sachs plan how they're going to make money in the coming decade, selling to the desperately poor probably isn't the first strategy that comes to mind. I can't really blame them. Although an old adage goes, "Sell to the rich, and live like the masses; sell to the masses and live like the rich," most investors don't think of the "masses" as people who live on just a dollar or two a day.

Generally, the people who have the greatest need for clean, sustainable electricity live in countries that struggle to attract stable long-term financial investment, which puts the countries and their people in a doubly bad situation. In addition to having largely low-income populations, some of these countries have also suffered from mercurial governments, natural disasters, wars, corruption, and even genocide. Often, women's rights are an afterthought, education is not where it should be, and health care is insufficient. All of these factors just heighten the funding challenge.[1]

A SWARM OF ACTIVITY

Hundreds of companies around the world are trying to tackle the problem and opportunity of bringing electricity to the 1.2. The market is extremely fragmented (almost pulverized, as one of my Duke University students put it) and immature. Despite this, these visionary businesspeople and NGOs are accomplishing a lot in the face of problems that many others would dismiss as insurmountable. Here are some of the key players along the value chain.

- *Design and production of portable solar lights and solar home systems, and pay-as-you-go cellular, cable, and keypad systems.* The established, relatively large players here include

Greenlight Planet, WakaWaka, Barefoot Power, Simpa, and d.light. Smaller companies include Off-Grid: Electric, Azuri, and Angaza. Multinationals working in the area include Philips and Schneider.

- *Distribution and retail sales, including traditional stores, roaming salespeople, partnerships, and leasing models.* These activities need to be developed, and ideally would be run largely by manufacturers, social enterprises, and NGOs. Despite valiant efforts and some relatively large investments in the tens of millions of dollars, none of the players in this market are as yet operating at scale. These include retailers such as the French company Total; social enterprises such as Off-Grid: Electric, Orb, WakaWaka, and M-KOPA; partnerships such as Orange S.A., Safaricom, and Duke Energy; and nonprofits such as Solar Sister, SunnyMoney, and the Global BrightLight Foundation.

- *Market supporters, including venture capitalists, governments, impact investors, and others.* There are a number of these, and I believe many more will step up to the plate as the effort progresses. Current players include the Omidyar Network, Gray Ghost, Acumen, the Shell Foundation, SunFunder, DFID, USAID, Lighting Global (The World Bank), GOGLA, the UN Foundation, and SE5ALL.[2]

ELECTRICITY IS A CAPITAL-INTENSE INDUSTRY

My years as an energy CEO, working on electricity projects in the US, Africa, Europe, and Latin America, have taught me that providing electricity is the most capital-intensive industry in the world. I was primarily developing massive grids and power plants, although I also raised capital for substantial wind, hydro, and solar projects. In the US, about 80 percent of power is provided by investor-owned utilities like Duke Energy, with the remainder supplied by municipal utilities and rural cooperatives. That's a sharp contrast to the low-income nations, most of which have state-controlled and state-financed utilities.

In the US, we have a complex collection of state and federal regulations that guide private investments in utilities. These guidelines say which types of private entities can access public financial markets to fund the infrastructure needed to supply electricity to all of a utility's customers. Other regulations mandate that US utilities supply electricity to every single person in their franchise area—including that "last mile" that can be so expensive to reach.

In return, state and federal governments generally grant the utilities a regulated monopoly over the area they service. In this way the government ensures that the utilities provide reliable service and universal access within their area at a reasonable cost. This practice was established in the early days of the twentieth century to encourage the electrification of America. This regulatory compact made it much easier for investors to put up money to finance the expansion of utilities.

Still, as successful as it is, this system only seemed to work well for urban centers, not the less accessible rural areas of the country, until the federal government stepped in and mandated universal access even for distant, isolated communities.

While Americans in the cities had power early in the twentieth century, one in ten US farmers went without electricity well into the 1930s. This disparity wasn't due to a lack of technology. Rather, it existed because there was more profit in supplying the cities than the rural areas. All this changed, however, when the federal government stepped in and mandated universal access with the Rural Electrification Act. Thank you, Franklin Delano Roosevelt. Passed in 1935, the Act guaranteed federal loans to expand power lines into rural areas. Consequently, cooperatives emerged to build single lines out to remote farms in rural areas. Co-ops bought power at a wholesale rate from the big utilities and then sold it to their members, the farmers and rural dwellers.

A NEW APPROACH

Right now there is very limited access to investment capital for the valiant people who are working so hard to bring sustainable power to rural areas of low-income countries. One of the keys to opening up this capital will be encouraging governments to establish local franchise areas for sustainable electrical companies to work within, which I discuss in more detail in chapter 10. But financing the effort is a complex task. Certainly, there's a vast difference between providing electricity in rural areas of the US in the 1930s and the challenge we now face of providing electricity to the 1.2. In general, the providers in rural areas in low-income countries are small companies with limited operating experience, and even more limited access to capital. Recently, Off-Grid: Electric and a few other companies have received millions of dollars in investments for their operations, but they are exceptions.

Consequently, the operations of these rural providers—and their ability to scale—suffer from limited working capital, which is another word for lack of adequate investment. I know I keep using the word "limited," but there's no way around it. Supplying electricity to rural areas is an immense challenge, given the current resources.

It doesn't help that some of the rural customers have few resources to pay for energy on any size or scale. Whether the power source is a small, relatively inexpensive solar lantern, a modest home solar kit, or a microgrid that can power several homes or even an entire village, often there is no money to pay for it—at least not up front. Some people still believe that it would be cheaper for the 1.2 in rural areas to purchase power from a new coal plant, but the reality is that they would never be able to afford to support the plant or the power lines. However, distributed solar generation offers people the chance to enter the electricity age on a small scale, and increase their access as they can better afford it.

This is where I think groups such as Practical Action, an organization in the UK dedicated to using technology to solve poverty, can teach us a great deal. Practical Action advocates splitting any problem they are trying to solve into categories of services or needs and tackling each one according to the unique opportunities and challenges it presents, based on people's ability to pay. Practical Action suggests that we develop and deploy strategies tailored to three categories of customers, including residential, community services (medical clinics and schools, for example), and productive enterprises.

Practical Action's theory is that each of these customer groups is key to the overall economic development of the community. This development will ultimately lead to an increase in the ability of the rural poor to pay for electricity and all that it makes possible. The idea is that as individuals prosper over time with access to electricity, their demand for electricity—and the devices and services it powers—will go up, creating a positive feedback loop within the local economy. Thus, while a family may only be able to afford a simple light to begin with, soon the elevation of the entire community will bring economic prosperity that will further electricity use and comfort. Next thing you know, the family that started with just a light will be looking at a low-energy refrigerator. This is a perfectly reasonable projection. But it's hard to sell investors on it, because it's not guaranteed.

Luckily, there are many possible creative solutions. For instance, one of the principal benefits of clean, sustainable electricity is that it makes kerosene—with all its attendant health risks from smoke and fire—redundant. Without any other options available, kerosene has been allowed to corner the rural power market. By going after the kerosene market, electrification offers a potentially large and as yet untapped revenue stream from carbon credits.

Because the new solar equipment would replace carbon-spewing fuel, it's possible that companies could earn carbon credits for every solar system installed. This is not as far-fetched as it seems. In 2012, a project that donated water filters to rural Kenyans was able to claim hundreds of thousands of carbon credits. The credits were earned because the people who used the water filters burned less wood to purify their water. The company then took those credits and sold them on the carbon market.[3] A similar reduction in carbon-emitting fuels happens when solar lights reduce the pollution from kerosene. Why not claim them? This is just one of the creative ways to approach the problem, and I think there are many other equally innovative solutions to be discovered.

Over time, business models that are structured to supply electricity to all three categories may have a better chance of being financed by traditional sources of capital.

OUR WORK CREATES ENTREPRENEURS

We have a big job ahead of us to school investors in the idea of rural electrification as a great human and economic development opportunity. Our job is made easier because the truth is that providing electricity leads to all sorts of benefits that the customer and community are willing to pay for. The investor gets both a return on investment and good will from associating with an important social enterprise. And everyone benefits from access to education, banking, and other areas, which, in turn, encourages investment by local entrepreneurs, bringing new jobs and economic improvements. The hope is that ultimately rural populations will move up along the road to the middle class. It may be quite a while before rural populations can realistically think about attaining a middle-class lifestyle. But they'll never think about it unless we get them more power.

How to deliver—and finance—rural electrification is even further complicated by the rearview mirror–focused programs run by powerhouse institutions like USAID and the Overseas Private Investment Corporation (OPIC), and the World Bank's program meant to end energy poverty. Historically, these prominent programs have spent the lion's share of their rural electrification money on massive central station generating plants controlled by state-owned enterprises. Distributed energy, where the power sources are small—such as solar panels—and spread throughout an area or community, is an afterthought, if anything.

Somehow, the conventional wisdom shared by these institutions is that it is cheaper to electrify rural areas by extending the grid in the traditional way. However, the facts of the modern world no longer bear out that assumption. We are in a changed landscape. There was no awareness of solar electricity in the 1930s. No one was concerned about climate change. Demand for power was not so acute.

These days, the cost of electricity from solar panels has fallen so precipitously that in low-income countries it is cheaper to deploy solar systems, and even microgrids, than it is to build new central station plants and run transmission and distribution networks into rural areas.[4] Three Indian states—Maharashtra, Delhi, and Kerala—all have found that off-grid solar, with no subsidies, was at parity with grid costs in 2013, and off-grid's price just keeps going down.[5] It's predicted that solar prices will drop a further 40 percent by 2017.

One thing that has not changed is the inability of the rural poor to pay for the huge cost of a grid. It would not be at all economically sustainable. On the other hand, there is every indication that people can afford to pay for distributed electricity that's generated at the household or village level via solar or other renewable-based systems. What is more, these systems can expand hand in hand with the wealth of the people who use them.

AS A START, A CONCERTED EFFORT needs to be made to change the allocation of capital by USAID, OPIC, and the World Bank. Right now, the US program called Power Africa is only using $1 billion of $7 billion allocated for the program for distributed, renewable generation in rural areas. I think much more of this money should flow to those underserved areas. We have to convince government agencies that they'll get more bang for every dollar invested in distributed energy generation than from grid-based systems. That will put more people on the road to an increased standard of living. It will also lead to the building of primarily renewable power systems, which will translate into carbon-free electricity and a growing commitment from the governments of these countries to start addressing the causes and the consequences of carbon change. These benefits will make a tremendous difference as we work to build a global consensus to mitigate the damage from carbon output.

One way of involving global economic development agencies would be to task them to develop criteria for future investment in off-grid electricity, whereby the agencies would offer investments on better terms to companies that operate in countries that have established off-grid franchises. Or the agencies could decide only to do business with these companies and countries. These incentives might have large influence.

And in fact, this is the exciting part. Since there are so few established electrical grids, we are free to invent the best solutions for the twenty-first century, from scratch. It's tougher to do that in the US, where solar has to compete with depreciated, lower-cost grids for investment and attention. (Whereas it would easily compete with a newly built, costly central station generation and transmission distribution system.) And the pushback from traditional utilities, seeking to ban solar and other distributed renewables from the American marketplace, has been fierce. In the low-income world, there's no such pushback.

ATTRACTING IMPACT INVESTORS

Today, high net-worth families and foundations in the US are studying how to invest their wealth and endowments in ways that will incentivize banks and other commercial investors to make a difference in the world (as well as a return). These impact investors could play a key role in financing electrification efforts.

Some experts believe that, so far, the funds available from impact investors are "more sizzle than steak," but I see these investors as potentially serious players in the US and international markets. Since 2000, Sir Ronald Cohen—an Egyptian-born British businessman who is sometimes called "the father of social investing"—and others from the UK have led the way in the development of innovative impact investment concepts. There are many funds dedicated to bringing about social change in the low-income world, of which electrification could certainly be a part.

I also believe universities that are looking to divest from investments associated with carbon output (a growing movement that is similar to the anti-apartheid movement of the 1980s) would perhaps be interested in pooling a portion of these resources into a fund for developing sustainable electricity. All of these impact investors would be looking at long-term, rather than short-term, gain. If a venture is successful, the impact investors would get their money back (and then some) in 10 to 20 years, when they could deploy it again on another worthy project. The investment also might help the impact investors achieve other goals related to education, health care, water, and sanitation, as all these areas improve with access to electricity.

Finally, I would like to see a concerted effort by foundations working in other areas, such as health care, gender equity, education, and social justice, to pool portions of investments from foundations to invest in rural electrification. I believe that support of electrification will be crucial to the success of each of these causes, so it's in everyone's interest to work together.

THE KEY TO SCALING ACCESS to electricity is the availability of low-cost capital. The franchise model, if designed appropriately, would create the certainty that investors need. The more the risk is reduced, and the greater the visibility of potential returns to investors, the lower the cost of capital. This will benefit both customers and investors. Recently, the International Finance Corporation released a report saying that poor people around the world spend more than $37 billion[6] a year on less-than-ideal energy sources, ranging from kerosene to cow dung, money that could be spent on sustainable energy, if it was available. Plus, a World Bank survey found access to electricity was among the most important concerns of entrepreneurs in the low-income world. There are billions of dollars in potential productivity from entrepreneurs who are unable to move ahead without electricity.

That's a lot of money that could be used to provide good service, improved standard of living, and profits in a virtuous cycle.

Fortunately, some international entrepreneurs are leading the way. Recently, Tony Elumelu, a Nigerian billionaire philanthropist, and Aliko Dangote, Africa's richest man, launched the African Energy Leaders Group (AELG) to encourage energy growth on the continent. An example of the large investments going into African countries is that a 2013 study found that over the previous six years the mobile phone industry in Sub-Saharan Africa raised $44 billion in commercial capital, while the off-grid electrical industry raised only $100 million. That's a paltry sum considering that people in the potential off-grid market in Sub-Saharan Africa are now spending about $10 billion a year on kerosene to light their homes. Africa is on the ascent, and Elumelu and Dangote, along with a group of fellow African billionaires, hope to drive investment and research into energy, including renewables.

This, more than anything, is the kind of financial involvement needed to make this plan work. And I know it's going to happen.

10

OVERCOMING BARRIERS
ON THE ROAD AHEAD

ON THE TIMELINE OF HUMAN ACHIEVEMENT, OUR MAS-
tery of electricity is very recent. Our early ancestors learned to control
fire about 800,000 years ago, possibly even earlier. Imagine how the
ability to cook, forge, and cast light—not to mention warm yourself
by a fire—has changed the world. Another vital tool, the wheel, was
invented about 5,500 years ago, changing the future of commerce,
warfare, and everything else we know.

In contrast, we only began providing electricity to the masses
about 130 years ago. We rapidly deployed electricity across the
Americas, Europe, Russia, Australia, and most other westernized
societies—but not everywhere on earth. Given electricity's impact
on culture, is it right to sit idly by while there are still 1.2 billion
people living in the dark? I don't believe it's an exaggeration to say
that the 1.2 are trapped in the distant past, living lives deprived of
modern conveniences. There's a bleak divide between the powerless
and those with power.

There are nearly four times as many people on earth without
power right now as there are people living in the entire United States.
Imagine that mass of people looking at the horizon every afternoon
to gauge when they have to return home to prepare dinner and clean

and do the washing before darkness falls. Imagine all those people shutting down for business when the sun goes down. It is hard to thrive without power.

About 85 percent of the 1.2 live in isolated, rural areas where they're unlikely to ever see a traditional grid power line. Curiously, many are connected to the larger world by mobile phone, as Sub-Saharan Africa has leapfrogged the analog age into the digital future. The rate of cell phone ownership in Nigeria and South Africa is the same as it is in the United States: 89 percent. The phones are used for texting, banking, talking to friends and family, and other purposes. I believe the 1.2 deserve full electrification, which will not only provide basic essentials such as light, but also allow them to charge computers and phones and watch TV, with all of those devices speaking to each other through the Internet of Things to regulate power usage to the most efficient degree.[1] And I believe all this power should be clean, sustainable energy that will keep this planet healthy. We need to bring clean power to every person on earth who desires it. No ifs, ands, or buts. It's that simple.

This effort will require many leaders. Many innovators—in technology, finance, government, and community building—will make it possible. The scale and scope will be unprecedented. But without it, our world will never be equitable, and we will continue down a path that is severely harmful to the future of our species. I am going to work tirelessly to make full, clean electrification happen, knowing that economic prosperity, good health, wisdom, and better government will flow from that work.

THE SUGAR WATER SOLUTION

In a perfect world, there would be many large, well-financed corporations focused on this issue, each of them facilitating low-cost supply chains, research and development of new technologies, and business models. These corporations would work with governments in many countries to mold and shape regulations to facilitate the development of off-grid electricity and minimize taxes and tariffs, which would make renewables cheaper for consumers. The majority of responsibility and authority for the work in a given country would be in the hands of citizens of that country.

I often think of the bright red-and-white labels on Coca-Cola bottles when I ponder access to electricity. Right now, Coca-Cola's ingenious supply chain gets bottles of Coke to nearly every village on earth—by truck, bike, and even camel—and then a few days later collects the bottles for reuse at a bottling plant. The company is guided by a corporate headquarters in Atlanta that oversees financing, product development, and marketing. Independent partners on the ground in some of the most remote areas of the world assure that Coca-Cola is present everywhere.

When I travel to places like Patagonia and China, I marvel at how this brand of flavored water has penetrated the global consciousness. I believe it's due to the following factors: consistency of product and design; marketing that speaks to broad populations but can be adapted to regional needs; and a bottling and distribution system that relies on local people and businesses. Coca-Cola has a sophisticated way of enriching local economies as well as the corporation itself that's a by-product of its supply chain. As strange as this may sound, since we're talking about a sweet drink with negative nutritional value, the profit Coca-Cola brings to many people during its long trip from factory to distant village gives the beverage an added feel-good element.

I believe that if Coca-Cola can get crates of its product to every community on earth each week (and in the areas that still use glass bottles pick up the empties for recycling), then we can get clean energy to the last villages at the end of every road and trail.

Along with this belief is the haunting specter of what's been called Coca-colonization—the thought that this giant corporation has imposed its American values wherever it's gone. Coca-colonization is part perception, and part reality. But in any event, it's clearly something to avoid in creating businesses that hope to help ensure that cultures around the world thrive.

The challenge right now is to get technology to the energy poor. Many companies and nonprofits are trying, but none of them are scaling quickly enough to even keep up with population growth, let alone make a measurable dent.

HOW TO SCALE

More than anything else, the key to scaling up access to energy is the creation of locally run franchises. These would be similar in many ways to the "territorial concessions in rural areas" that have been made to private companies in Senegal, Brazil, and elsewhere. These give exclusive rights to an area in order to encourage investment and service. I also look to the American experience of providing energy access for some insight into the future of access in low-income countries. Considering the American success with regulated natural monopolies, the need for governmental intervention, and the shift in the availability and cost of renewables such as solar as compared to traditional centralized power generation, I believe the key to financing starts with government establishment of locally run franchises. Locally owned and operated franchises will help combat the handicaps that plague small start-ups, which not only have limited experience and capital, but also must compete for market share. These franchises will be mini monopolies, smaller-scale versions of what led to American electrification in the twentieth century. These rural franchises will be operated contiguously with state-owned utilities.

Taking away the burden of competing and allowing economies of scale to flourish will remove many of the barriers to bringing electricity access to scale. The difference will be that the franchises granted in low-income countries will be for rural initiatives, as opposed to monopolies for servicing highly populated areas, like those in the US. To prevent abuses in a monopolistic franchise system, which by its nature will favor one supplier over all others, governments would need to establish regulations that would include performance standards to assure that the right technology is deployed, that it is properly maintained, and that it is fairly priced. Companies could compete for the right to a franchise through an auction.

With the exclusive right to serve, companies could build bankable business plans, raise capital, and plan for the deployment of technologies to bring electricity to rural customers at the least cost, and to scale. The deployment plan would include specific scenarios for scaling access as communities grow and people's ability to pay increases. The benefit of the franchise approach would be that the energy provider would develop a deep understanding of its customers as well as an understanding of the economic opportunities that it could grasp, and would be able to manage marketing, deployment, financing, maintenance and repairs, expansion of individual systems or village-wide solutions, and billing in an efficient manner, as opposed to the current patchwork approach. After winning a franchise, a provider would be able to use its market share to attract investors, thereby building capital. The customers would win because a larger provider with more capital available to finance deployment would make it possible for the customer base to pay off the systems over time, or lease the systems, rather than paying for them outright.

Plus, with a provider rooted in the community for the long term, customers would feel secure knowing there'd be someone to repair or replace their system if needed. And everyone would benefit as the local economy grew. By granting franchises in the US in the early twentieth century we were able to accelerate the provision of access at a lower cost, and I think we could repeat that process in low-income countries, this time focusing on rural, rather than urban areas. Thus, while solving the financing problem, we would also be creating a public-private approach to solving the access issue in the rural areas.

This approach would lead to the consolidation of the many companies pursuing rural electrification today. There might be some resistance from some companies, but I think that overall the increased access to capital, technology, design, and marketing would be attractive to many of the players. Consolidation would create companies with stronger, bigger balance sheets. The ability to create business models that scale would also be a consequence of this consolidation. Purchasing advantages—reduced costs for solar panels, inverters, and payment systems—would lead to a reduction in costs to consumers as well as increased profits. Banks and impact investors would respond well to this.

TECHNOLOGY

With locally run franchises and financing (which were covered in more depth in chapter 9) in place, another pillar is the involvement of local leaders and employees. We are very fortunate to be developing our ideas at a time of unprecedented technological innovation and creativity. It sometimes seems as if there is no problem that will not be solved by a smart kid with an app. We are on the cusp of a huge shift wherein technological and manufacturing improvements put the cost of solar generation on par with—and in some cases even cheaper than—traditional power-generating methods such as coal and gas. Battery capacity and storage life are also increasing exponentially. These improvements are quickly making solar an even more viable option for 24/7 power.

The popular belief that renewable energy is too expensive to gain wide acceptance can no longer be justified. This change will upset the apple cart, as people used to say before they started saying "disruptive."

WE KNOW BY NOW that the traditional grid, powered by traditional fuels, is not the solution to getting power to the poor. It's too dirty, expensive, and unreliable. Instead of building coal plants that send electricity out over copper wires, we're going to increase the penetration of affordable, well-designed, decentralized, off-grid technologies—what we in the business call distributed electricity generation.

Right now, solar is the best choice even though it is not reliable 24/7. But eventually, wind, hydro, biomass, biofuels, and other energy sources, such as fuel cells, will almost certainly play a role. The fuels for solar power, wind, and hydro are free. That means that if the electricity is distributed locally, there will be very few costs, other than the equipment—such as solar panels for solar power, turbines for hydropower, and local distribution infrastructure, when necessary—that is used to collect and convert the free energy. This will be a key to success.

The type of technology used in a given situation will depend on the size and needs of the community, its location, and the weather, as well as people's ability to pay. I expect that having an anchor customer, such as a small business, school, or medical clinic, will be a big help in getting the community on board. Of course, an anchor customer would also help in the financing of the project, and serve as a catalyst for getting electricity into the rest of the community.

The basic tech choices available right now form a ladder of options, ranging from simple low-light lamps to really bright ceiling fixtures, with fans, radios, televisions, and computers added to the mix. Although some experts maintain that the World Bank has a more sophisticated approach to describing the range of options available as electricity scales, I still believe this simpler approach is better. The first rung on the ladder is the inexpensive solar lantern with a built-in battery, various types of which have been distributed for free or sold all over the world, to great effect. The next rung is a solar lantern that also charges cell phones. One rung up from that is the home solar system, in which a solar panel on the roof is used to charge several lights, with a phone charger attached, and a central battery system to hold the charge at night. These systems can vary widely, with some being powerful enough to run a blender or even a TV. At the top of the ladder right now is the microgrid, discussed in chapter 8. These microgrids can offer full electrification to a village, and also provide sophisticated monitoring systems that track energy use and battery life.

Of course, the price goes up on the higher rungs, and price is perhaps the most important consideration in this arena. In many cases, we are talking about people who live on less than two dollars a day—often much less. Any effort to bring power to rural areas must respect the reality of people's limited finances. People who might not have access to toilets, who have to walk great distances for water and firewood, and who sometimes struggle to obtain sufficient food are by necessity cautious with their money. For them, an outlay of $10 is significant, and not something they would easily risk.

FORM AND FUNCTION

Until recently, no one gave much consideration to holistic design of distributed energy for the 1.2. How the light functions and what it costs have thus far been the only considerations. The result has been a bunch of ungainly lamps and awkwardly designed solar panels. They have no marketing value as objects beyond the fact that they give light. There is nothing about them that says, "Buy me." I think we can do better, and must, if we are to attract people to the products and give them an incentive to integrate these products into their lives. The poverty of the consumer should not affect the quality of the design. In fact, it makes design all the more important, given that any object becomes more precious to someone who has very little.

This may seem a strange luxury, but innovative product design will be central to any effort to electrify the world. To accomplish this, I would recommend that companies that are providing electricity establish a central design laboratory dedicated to distributed energy with as much focus as Apple dedicated to the iPod and the iPhone. We need equipment that is modular and elegant. That way, the equipment can be customized to fit the needs of a particular region or customer, and broken parts can be removed and replaced by the customer or service agent.

Modular design also solves a huge problem that traditional utilities call "stranded costs." Stranded costs are the debt incurred by a utility when it installs a large-scale and tremendously expensive technology that then becomes obsolete before the end of its useful life, and before the costs to build it have been recovered. The equipment is useless, but the debt remains. With modular equipment, stranded costs are a much smaller risk. That risk goes down further if modules are designed to incorporate new technologies that will allow the equipment to be easily updated.

The equipment design has to be attractive, highly intuitive, and useful. For instance, great care has to be taken to ensure that the quality of light projected from the lamp is good, and that the lamp looks good even when it is turned off. The equipment also must be easy to use. Hanging lights must have shades to reflect the light downward. These requirements may seem simple, but they would be a big improvement over most of the lamps out there. The batteries should be as small as possible, held in containers that will look good in someone's home, and the switches and wires should be designed for functionality and appearance.

Most everyone likes to have a nice home, no matter their income level, and our efforts should reflect these basic human desires. Every thought that goes into this mission should focus on enhancing people's day-to-day lives. People will want these products if they actually add something to their lives.

Consumer technology also plays a key role in the expansion and acceptance of off-grid energy. We must emphasize and inform customers about the great potential of highly efficient appliances to enrich their lives. There are millions of people waiting for the right efficient products for their homes; I don't think this will be a difficult sell. For too long the emphasis in rural electrification has been on just lighting the home. While this has been a revolutionary change, technology is now reaching the point where we can also introduce highly efficient televisions, refrigerators, computer tablets, and other appliances that will work with home solar systems and microgrids.

As time goes on, the factories to produce all of this equipment should be located in the countries that consume the items. Again, this will add to the positive feedback loop that is central to this effort.

SALES AND DISTRIBUTION

The final pillar of this endeavor—and perhaps the most daunting task besides financing—is establishing the on-the-ground sales and service teams. Providing off-grid power is a labor intensive, people-centered enterprise. This effort must be done with local people, as much as possible. Each culture and area of a country may have a different make-up, with different electrical needs and distinct ways of doing business. The best way to respect this is by employing people who are part of and fluent in the culture, and who can inspire trusting relationships. Establishing a clean energy education campus in each country will be essential to this effort.

These power schools would attract the leading lights and entrepreneurs from the population to learn, and then lead the way, in their regions. And these students would give us, and the local entrepreneurs leading the effort on the ground, invaluable information about what the electrical needs are, and what marketing and installation methods work best in each area.

Other companies have tried similar efforts with good success. Off-Grid: Electric, in Tanzania, has a school that offers in-house training to bright Tanzania students, with the idea that they'll join the company afterward if they are a good fit. And my friends at Practical Action told me about their training center in Peru, which has supplied many skilled people to install micro-hydro projects in that country.

OWNERSHIP AND PURCHASING ENERGY SERVICES

Consumer purchase and ownership of the power systems is a key to our plan's success. Over the last few years I have spoken to many people who are involved with distributing solar equipment to people who lack it. Almost without fail, they have shared lessons about the value of ownership. It seems that purely charitable gifts of equipment are not valued as much by the recipients as equipment in which they have a financial stake. I believe people have to either own what they use, or pay for the electricity they consume. The further people are able to climb up the ladder on their own, the more they will transition from buying products like a solar lantern to paying for an electricity service, such as from a microgrid.

This would not apply to health clinics, schools, and other similarly vital community centers. Franchises would be required to offer electricity to these locations at a small profit or at cost, or even less if the government can be convinced to subsidize the program. These venues could also offer free phone charging to those who needed it. This has a humanitarian side, but it is also a calculated business move: locations offering phone-charging become anchors for the community, showing everyone the value of electricity.

I know the idea of making money off the poor can sound heartless. Applying capitalist sensibilities to the business of providing power to some of the world's poorest citizens can seem completely contrary to the mission of getting electricity to the last village at the end of the road. However, in case after case I've found that lights last longer and are better cared for when the customer either buys the equipment or pays for the power. One notable exception in which strictly charitable work makes sense is in the refugee camps, where people are absolutely unable to pay for anything.

Ownership keeps the solar company sustainable in a way that pure charity can never do. Our Global BrightLight Foundation operates with a hybrid system. In refugee camps we give the lights away, but in other places we try to make a profit, which we reinvest in more solar lanterns for more people. This helps make the system economically sustainable, and that is the key to long-term success.

PAYMENT

Pay as you go is another model. This is less common, but quite successful in many ways, and has been implemented by Off-Grid: Electric in Tanzania, and by other companies in other countries. I prefer it. In this model, the company supplies, installs, and maintains the equipment, sometimes requesting a small monthly fee, sometimes not. The customer pays in advance for a certain amount of power, using it as they wish.

I propose a new kind of utility model to supplant the traditional model. Traditionally, a company like Duke Energy incurs all the fuel and infrastructure costs, including building new generating plants and power lines, and maintenance. The customer uses as much electricity as they want, and pays at the end of the month. The customer's payment for electricity goes up across the board when the utility has high infrastructure expenses due to upgrades or when usage increases during extreme weather or when the fuel costs rise. The model I propose puts the parent company in charge of marketing, design, financing, and other factors, while establishing local consortiums that build out infrastructure in villages in their region, using the standardized, adaptable equipment supplied by the parent company. This ensures local control over the production and consumption of electricity, which I think is vital to the long-term success of this project. The local utility maintains all the equipment and collects money on a pay-as-you-go basis.

Payment is probably the most evolved aspect of this equation. Because most people in low-income countries have cell phones, mobile banking has taken off in a way that is hard to imagine in the United States. Because of this, the simplest system would have the customer send a mobile payment of cash for a certain amount of electricity. In turn, they would receive a code that they could enter into their home system, releasing electricity from their batteries or the neighborhood microgrid for a set period of time.

Curiously, this payment aligns with the customer's existing relationship to purchasing kerosene for light. Most people in low-income countries purchase kerosene as needed, a small amount at a time, because they lack the capital to easily purchase more. Mobile payment mirrors this same financial relationship, substituting solar power for archaic kerosene. This ease aligns the customer's need for light on demand with the company's need for payment.

MOBILE RULES

Mobile banking is definitely becoming the dominant financial force in rural areas. That's in contrast to the disappointing results of some innovative financial services offered to the same populations in recent years. A good example is the much hyped business of microloans to the poor, which seemed to hold great promise but has proved to have a more mixed track record.

Until recently, the concept of microloans, such as those given by Grameen Bank and others, has been widely praised. Hundreds of millions of people have borrowed small amounts from these banks. But a close look at these efforts will show that they come up short. Most striking, the high cost of granting these loans and collecting payments leads to sometimes-usurious interest rates, which is not good for anyone. And though the original idea was to give people, especially women, the chance to build small businesses and grow economically, numerous studies have shown there's little evidence that the loans help lift large numbers of people out of poverty.

However, the high penetration of mobile phones into the market might change this, because phone-based banking tools make banking cheaper and hence more accessible for poor people. A recent survey found that over half of all people in a group of Sub-Saharan countries had sent money to another person via mobile phones in the previous weeks. While microlenders in these countries struggle to reach 10 percent market penetration, 62 percent of Kenyan adults and 47 percent of Tanzanian adults are mobile money users, according to a report in *Foreign Affairs*. That high market penetration allowed one mobile money company, M-Pesa, to do $12 billion worth of transactions in the first half of 2013 alone. The company also does nearly a billion dollars of transactions a year in neighboring Tanzania. This is proof that phones work well as banking centers. Clearly, mobile payment is the best way to handle financial transactions between the customer and the off-grid utility.[2]

The really brilliant effects will be apparent when cell phones, access to electricity, and mobile banking all come together. At that point we will truly be in a new age. Let's do it!

IMPEDIMENTS

Now for a dose of reality. This plan is great in theory, but in practice there will be many financial and political hurdles to overcome. Honestly, I kind of like that. I've been battling sometimes-intractable bureaucracies, and persuading doubtful financial analysts and bankers, for years. I worry I'd get complacent without the challenge.

We will face five basic barriers in bringing clean energy to the 1.2:

- Consumer trust, because of one poorly executed idea or dishonest businessperson can make consumers unwilling to risk their hard-earned money on an unknown product. To overcome this we'd have to establish worldwide lighting and equipment quality standards, and develop close relationships with customers, local brands, and community, religious, and political organizations.

- Low levels of disposable income that make paying for solar-powered lights or solar home systems difficult for energy-poor people. The declining cost of solar hardware, the improvement of software, and the rise in pay-as-you-go models should ease this burden.

- Initial low returns won't interest traditional venture capitalists, and impact investors tend to focus on distributors and manufacturers, so there's limited investment available to start research and development before the revenue starts flowing. We might encourage impact-focused accelerator programs and incubators, a model that has worked well elsewhere.

- The local distributors will need short-term debt in order to grow their inventories, but local banks are too expensive. Perhaps crowdsourcing opportunities could help with this issue.

- Import restrictions and government subsidy policies discourage the marketplace, so we'd need to work with governments and NGOs to ease these impediments.

All the technology in the world will be less than useless without the cooperation of governments and access to capital.[3] There are several key political roadblocks that must be eliminated, and incentives that must be created. These include:

- Making it easier to import solar panels, lanterns, and other necessary technology, and the infrastructure for building microgrids. This will keep costs down for the rural poor.

- Governments will have to adopt policies that encourage the deployment of solar lanterns and solar home systems and microgrids. I would encourage governments to establish regulatory agencies dedicated to this effort.
- The subsidies for kerosene will have to be reduced or eliminated. This is a huge ask of any government in which the kerosene industry has a strong lobbying effort. And I think one way to get rid of subsidies will be to co-opt the kerosene industry by encouraging them to invest in solar deployment.

Regarding incentives, here are two proactive steps that must be taken:

- Governments will have to adopt and enforce solar photovoltaics quality standards so the inferior product doesn't flood the market, undermining superior products.
- Governments need to establish rural franchise areas—local monopolies—that will be bid on and controlled by private companies, as sole suppliers. As with US utilities, this guarantee would come with obligations. In this case, the parent company would be required to offer universal access, fair pricing, and speedy deployment. The parent company would also be required to use local companies and labor.

Corruption can be a huge issue. Overcoming corruption can require actions to both eliminate certain practices as well as to implement new practices, standards, penalties, or enforcement measures.

The problem of corruption presents itself when a corrupt government—and sadly there are plenty of them—puts pressure on the local utility division to participate in its corrupt ways. If the government is in charge of licensing the utilities' activities, the pressure could be very intense.

My answer would be to create a public-private regulatory model that governments could adapt in areas where large numbers of people have no access to electricity. This will be a difficult endeavor, but it is necessary and could possibly provide benefits beyond the electrification effort as a model for battling corruption generally.

Another issue that deserves attention is that, because many countries now are working to extend their traditional grids, agreements would need to be struck with those entities to ensure that they would reimburse either the parent company or the local utility (these entities are interchangeable for these purposes) for any expenses that were incurred by the franchisee to install a microgrid that was later connected and adopted into their systems. Rules would need to be created so that villages could continue to use the system put into place by the franchisee if that electricity were cheaper, and/or could sell any excess power to the traditional grid-based system that it could use either for the village or to transmit to other users.

FINALLY, TO ACCELERATE AND strengthen the electrification effort, I'd work to designate access to electricity as a basic human right by the United Nations and would include access to electricity as one of the sustainable development goals being established for the next 15 years. By elevating access to electricity in this way, the low-income countries could more easily make it one of their top priorities and justify allocating resources to the effort as well as work to establish the appropriate regulatory environment. Such status would make it easier for those who have the ability to scale the effort to convince governments to adopt the goals and measures I've outlined.

PRACTICAL ACTION

I was fortunate enough to travel to the UK to meet with the key representatives of a highly effective organization called Practical Action. This organization's mission is to "use technology to challenge poverty in developing countries." It focuses on several key areas, including food, water, health, and climate change. The organization has done a wonderful job of addressing the impediments to providing universal energy access around the world.

This international charity (and its predecessor) has been working for 50 years to address the challenges of poverty around the world. Based on its grassroots experience, it provides consulting services, publishes articles about issues, and advocates for policies that will improve the lives of poor people everywhere.

One morning I drove north from London's city center for an hour and a half to Practical Action's base in Rugby. There I met with Aaron Leopold and Dr. Lucy Stevens, along with a few others. I was very familiar with their work, having used it in a course on energy access that I co-taught at Duke University with Professor Tim Profeta, director of the Nicholas Institute for Environmental Policy

Solutions at Duke, of which I am a board member. The publication we used focused on the residential, community, and business uses of electricity.

Leopold and Stevens were confident that even with the urbanization that is occurring in the world the rural challenge will not go away. They also strongly believe that one of the keys to successful deployment is convincing poor people in rural areas that off-grid technologies are not second best, and are actually the leading twenty-first-century technologies to provide affordable energy services. I wholeheartedly agree.

Practical Action had also observed that it is important to build capacity at all levels within low-income countries. To achieve this, the group believes we need to overcome the bias that favors investments in traditional utilities—generation, transmission, and distribution—rather than in off-grid projects. This bias exists in most low-income countries, as well as most financial institutions.

What I like about Practical Action, and why I offer it as an example of success, is that it has implemented workable solutions for complicated problems. The organization has done this by understanding the culture of whatever region it is in, and working to understand what solutions will actually meet the needs and preferences of the people there.

Having seen the results that this organization has achieved, I would recommend a global strategy that works with Practical Action and similar groups to encourage governments to establish a model set of laws that pave the way for franchises. The model laws would be based on research, incorporating the incentives and regulations described above, and would encourage the appropriate technologies, as well as meet the needs of local communities. These would start as "one size fits all" regulations that could then be adapted to fit local mores and customs. But the lead idea is that governments would receive the answers they needed up front on how the technology works and would be deployed, and those governments, in turn, could plug the standards into their regulatory systems as appropriate.

THE LANDSCAPE IS CHALLENGING

The hard reality is that the financial math of providing off-grid electricity in rural areas is damn difficult. I would compare the task ahead to the task of setting up a grid in the US. The US power sector is the most capital-intensive industry in the country. You'd think it would be a lot cheaper to bring off-grid power to low-income countries, but that isn't the case. When looked at in terms of the size of their economies and the limited ability of customers to pay, it's equally capital intensive. And it is very difficult to finance. The model I suggest would solve many of these problems.

Large investors are wary of the off-grid industry because it is generally composed of small companies with limited experience and capital, none of which dominate their markets to a great degree. Clearly, an effort with a global scope would be more appealing.

In addition to creating a regulatory model that would inspire all the in-country efforts around the world, this approach would lead to the consolidation of companies within sectors in each area. This would give us a bigger scale, stronger balance sheets, much more ease in attracting capital, and marketing power.

I believe that, with these efforts, the world will see full rural electrification as a real possibility in the next decade, and a visible fact in the next 15 years. That will be the definition of our success.

ACKNOWLEDGMENTS

MANY PEOPLE GAVE ME GREAT SUPPORT, INSIGHT, AND encouragement as I wrote this book.

Rye Barcott, my colleague and friend at Duke Energy, who is now a founder and managing partner at Double Time Capital, helped me launch this project with sage advice about agents, editors, and all the steps in between. His help was invaluable as I made the transition from being the chairman and CEO of Duke Energy to writing this book.

No book succeeds without a thoughtful literary agent, and I was lucky to have Katherine Flynn of the Kneerim, Williams & Bloom agency in Boston. She inspired and informed my thinking every step of the way. Most important, she steered me toward St. Martin's Press, where senior editor Emily Carleton has been supportive and helpful from the start. I am thankful that she believed we must inspire many others in order to solve the challenge of providing electricity to the 1.2 billion with no access. Her confidence in the project gave me strength.

I am full of gratitude for the opportunity to work with Stephen P. Williams. He is a terrific writer. Equally important, he is fun, irreverent, and a great guy to hang out with—my highest compliment for a partner. Our contrasting skills and experiences complemented each other well, and together we tried to discover the best way for the world to help more than a billion people lift themselves out of poverty with access to electricity. Thanks also to his agent, Madeleine Morel, of 2M Communications, for introducing us.

I want to thank Tim Profeta, director of the Nicholas Institute for Environmental Policy Solutions at Duke University, who co-taught a course with me at Duke. Our students there had robust discussions about many of the ideas in this book. The students represented five different graduate schools—engineering, law, business, public policy, and environmental science—and their critical thinking was invaluable to the growth of my ideas. Every class Tim and I taught boosted my confidence in the future of our country and the world. These young people are smart and thoughtful. An environmental lawyer named Tatjana Vujic worked right alongside Tim and me. She helped us shape the direction of the course and, most important, she reviewed this book and offered many suggestions as how best to shape the narrative.

I am also indebted to Joe Hale, a friend and business associate for more than 25 years. In December 2010, we were discussing the energy access challenge when we decided to explore starting a foundation to provide solar lanterns in remote areas of the world. In 2011, we created the Global BrightLight Foundation and were off and running. We have either distributed philanthropically or sold more than 70,000 solar lanterns that also charge cell phones in rural areas of the world. It's been a satisfying and challenging process to help people change their lives with access to clean, reliable energy. This process deepened my curiosity about how best to accelerate the provision of electricity and spurred me to write this book.

John Stowell, my good friend and decades-long business associate, has been invaluable in moving the issue of access to power for the rural poor to the forefront. A former newspaper reporter and excellent communicator and writer, John was great at building coalitions of people to work on this issue. He was instrumental in getting the Global Sustainable Electricity Partners to focus their efforts, and as a board member of the Global BrightLight Foundation, helped us succeed in ways that otherwise wouldn't have been possible.

Many people supported my efforts writing this book, but Kathy Currence was the one who made every detail of the project work. She's a miracle worker. We have been working together almost a decade, and she has had to learn to deal with my inability to say no to new opportunities and speeches. I appreciate her almost inexhaustible patience with me.

I owe a great debt to the pioneering work of the people of Practical Action, who for more than 50 years have been addressing the issues affecting low-income people around the world, including energy access. My conversations with Aaron Leopold and Dr. Lucy Stevens gave me invaluable insights into the challenges we face in providing electricity to people in the rural parts of our planet. Their thoughtful observations in *Poor People's Energy Outlook for 2014* framed the issues we face. I also used the report when I co-taught a graduate course at Duke University entitled Renewable Energy and the World's Poor in the fall of 2014.

While researching this book, I relied on the pioneering work of Bob Freling, executive director of the Solar Electric Light Fund, or SELF, in Washington, DC. He has been a leader in energy access for more than 20 years. Bob was the first to make a compelling argument that access to electricity should be designated a basic human right by the UN. He also believed that the UN failed when they didn't make access a Millennium Development Goal in 2000. He properly believes that these steps would prod countries with low per capita income to make bringing electricity to its citizens a priority.

I have also been blessed to have had insightful conversations with many other people who shared their passion for solving the energy access challenge, including people from NGOs, start-ups, and established companies; government leaders from Sub-Saharan Africa, India, and Latin America; the United States Agency for International Development, the World Bank, and the team from the UN—Sustainable Energy for All. Thanks to all of you.

Many dedicated people helped further the research for this book in Africa, India, and elsewhere. My heartfelt thanks to Sam Dargan, founder of Great Lakes Energy, in Rwanda, and the Global BrightLight Foundation's partner on the ground in that country. He was an insightful and engaging guide. Amir Hirwa, of the United Nations High Commissioner for Refugees (UNHCR), was generous with his time and guidance at the Kiziba Refugee Camp, administered by the UNHCR. Thanks also to Mike Hughes, an adviser to the Rwanda Ministry of Education and one of the founders of the Rwanda UK Goodwill Organization (or RUGO), for his expertise and introductions, including to Consolee Uwibambe, vice mayor of the Kayonza district in Rwanda. My thanks to the very gracious solar engineers Odette Mukaromongi, Claudine Ubelimana, Cecile Nyiramuban, and Dative Mukantabana for allowing access to the work they've done in Karambi, Rwanda.

In Uganda, Becca Schwartz, the business development director for Solar Sister, was gracious and informative, and a lot of fun. Many thanks to Becca and her coworker, Jayne Opitto, the sales manager for Solar Sister in Uganda, for their guidance. And this connection wouldn't have happened, of course, without the efforts of Katherine Lucey, who founded Solar Sister and remains the guiding force.

Off-Grid:Electric, based in Arusha, Tanzania, offered an eye-opening tour of their innovative approach to providing solar power to East Africa. Many thanks to their CEO, Xavier Hegelson, and his team, especially to Raphael Robert, for sharing his story. Finally, Senguku Ali, a driver and guide based in Kampala, Uganda, was an invaluable member of the team in Rwanda and Uganda.

In India, Bunker Roy and his dedicated colleagues offered insights, advice, and awesome vegetarian food at the campus of Barefoot College in Tilonia, Rajasthan. Thank you to the women solar engineers in residence who offered much wisdom and many anecdotes about their experiences. In Kolkata, Sudipta Dawn, the general manager for operations for ONergy, was a tireless guide and made countless valuable introductions in West Bengal. My heartfelt thanks to Krish Krishnan, founder of Green Villages, for making his team members available on a moment's notice for a visit to villages and homes in the state of Uttar Pradesh. This was an eye-opening experience. Rakesh Sharma, based in New Delhi, was an indefatigable guide and driver, who smoothed every interaction and made every wish come true. Thank you.

Finally, I'd like to thank my family. I am blessed to have three caring children—Chrissi Morgan, Kara Black, and Benjamin Rogers. I am grateful for the way they have enriched and helped shape my life.

In the end, my truest thanks go to my closest confidant, my wife MA (known as Mary Anne to her family), who provided unflagging encouragement. She has stood by me through my many and varied reinventions through the years, offering solidity, insight, and a lot of patience. She graciously supported this latest adventure with an unfailing sense of humor when I found myself becoming terminally serious.

I have dedicated this book to my eight grandchildren because they are the barometers for all that I do. For several decades, I have made decisions based on the grandchildren's test—meaning, what effect will today's decision have on the lives of others long after I'm gone? It's a tough test—when they are my age and look back on my life, will the decisions I made when they were young still seem like good decisions? I hope so.

Jim Rogers
Charlotte, North Carolina

NOTES

PROLOGUE

1. "SE4ALL Global Tracking Framework," The World Bank, http://www
.worldbank.org/en/topic/energy/publication/Global-Tracking-Framework
-Report.
2. World Energy Outlook, 2014, http://www.worldenergyoutlook.org/publica
tions/weo-2014/.

CHAPTER 2 : DARKNESS VISIBLE

1. "Idi Amin Quotes," BrainyQuote, http://www.brainyquote.com/quotes/quo
tes/i/idiamin556179.html.
2. data.worldbank.org/indicator/EG.ELC.ACCS.ZS.
3. "Illegal Electricity Connections Claim Ten Lives in Mbale," URN, December 5, 2008, https://ugandaradionetwork.com/a/story.php?s=19384.
4. "Kasese Takes Lead on CleanEnergy Campaign," *The Observer,* August 27,
2013, http://www.observer.ug/index.php?option=com_content&view=arti
cle&id=27190:kasese-takes-lead-on-clean-energy-campaign.
5. "Uganda Overview," The World Bank, http://www.worldbank.org/en/cou
ntry/uganda/overview. "Death Trap at Home," *New Vision,* http://www.new
vision.co.ug/mobile./Detail.aspx?NewsID=644035&CatID=396.
6. Observations throughout are based on Stephen P. Williams' experience and
conversations in Uganda.
7. Statistic is based on electrification rate of less than 10 percent. https://
energypedia.info/wiki/Electrifying_Africa:_Grid_Extension_Models_in
_Sub-Saharan_Africa#Tanzania:_A_Young_REA_Approach.
8. Based on interview by Stephen P. Williams.
9. Tina Rosenberg, "The Next Wireless Revolution, in Electricity," Fixes, *New
York Times,* September 11, 2013, http://opinionator.blogs.nytimes.com/2013
/09/11/the-next-wireless-revolution-in-light/?_r=0.
10. Andrew Webb, "5 Reasons Why We Should Kill Off Kerosene Lamps for
Good," Generation Change, The Blog, *The Huffington Post,* November 13,
2014, http://www.huffingtonpost.com/andrew_webb/5-reasons-why-we-sh

     ould-k_b_5869166.html and http://nextbillion.net/blogpost.aspx?blogid=1 571.

11. James Melik, "Solutions Sought to End Use of Kerosene Lamps," *BBC News Business,* September 26, 2012, http://www.bbc.com/news/business -18262217. Sarah Yang, "Let There Be Clean Light: Kerosene Lamps Spew Black Carbon, Should Be Replaced, Study Says," UC Berkeley News Center, November 28, 2012, http://newscenter.berkeley.edu/2012/11/28/kerosene -lamps-black -carbon/.

12. Ibid.

13. "Impact," SolarAid, http://www.solar-aid.org/impact.

14. http://newscenter.berkeley.edu/2012/11/28/kerosene-lamps-black-carbon/.

15. Webb, "5 Reasons Why We Should Kill Off Kerosene Lamps for Good."

16. "Lamp Topples, 2 Kids Burnt to Death," *The Times of India,* February 6, 2011, http://timesofindia.indiatimes.com/city/kolkata-/Lamp-topples-2-kids -burnt-to-death/articleshow/7434340.cms?referral=PM.

17. "2012 India Blackouts," *Wikipedia,* http://en.wikipedia.org/wiki/2012_India _blackouts. "Demographics of Uttar Pradesh," *Wikipedia,* http://en.wiki pedia.org/wiki/Demographics_of_Uttar_Pradesh.

18. Based on Stephen P. Williams' reporting in India and elsewhere.

CHAPTER 3: FROM THE COAL
MINE TO THE COFFEE POT

1. "Household Air Pollution and Health," Media Centre, World Health Organization, March 2014, http://www.who.int/mediacentre/factsheets/fs292/en.

2. Dan Jaffe, Sofya Malashanka, Greg Hof, Jeff Thayer, and Justin Putz, "Do Coal and Diesel Trains Make for Unhealthier Air?" http://www.atmos .washington.edu/jaffegroup/modules/APOLLO/. "The Dirty Truth about Coal Dust," Sierra Club, http://action.sierraclub.org/site/DocServer/100_158 _CoalDust_FactSht_04_X1A__2_.pdf?docID=12643.

3. https://www.youtube.com/watch?v=r_1T2_143Xo.

CHAPTER 4: THE INNOVATIVE SUPPLIERS

1. Observations throughout chapter based on reporting in India and Africa by Stephen P. Williams.

2. www.rugo.org.

3. SolarSister (website), http://www.solarsister.org.

CHAPTER 5: ELECTRICITY IN THE WORLD

1. "Addressing Haiti's Energy Challenges: A Key Priority in the Years to Come," The World Bank, September 25, 2012, http://www.worldbank.org /en/news/feature/2012/09/25/energy-supply-haiti.

2. "Haiti—NOTICE: Electricity and Matches of the World Cup 2014," *Haiti Libre,* http://www.haitilibre.com/en/news-11354-haiti-notice-electricity-and -matches-of-the-world-cup-2014.html.

3. "Energy in Japan," *Wikipedia,* https://en.wikipedia.org/wiki/Energy_in_Japan.

4. "Energy-Elecitricity-Production: Countries Compared," *Nationmaster,* http://www.nationmaster.com/country-info/stats/Energy/Electricity/Production.

5. "China to Lead in New Nuclear Reactors?" *Nuclear Power Daily,* October 11, 2011, http://www.nuclearpowerdaily.com/reports/China_to_lead_in_new_nuclear_reactors_999.html.

6. "China and Coal," *Sourcewatch,* http://www.sourcewatch.org/index.php?title=China_and_coal.

7. "Coal Gasification," *Wikipedia,* http://en.wikipedia.org/wiki/Coal_gasification; "China to Build 50 Coal Gasification Facilities," Institute for Energy Research, August 6, 2014, http://instituteforenergyresearch.org/analysis/china-build-50-coal-gasification-facilities/.

8. Christine Ottery, "China's Planned Coal-to-Gas Plants to Emit over One Billion Tons of CO_2," http://www.greenpeace.org/international/en/news/features/China-coal-to-gas-plants-to-emit-billion-tons-of-CO2/; Edward Wong, "China's Energy Plans Will Worsen Climate Change, Greenpeace Says," *New York Times,* July 23, 2014, http://www.nytimes.com/2014/07/24/world/asia/greenpeace-says-chinas-energy-plans-exacerbate-climate-change.html?partner=rss&emc=rss&module=Search&mabReward=relbias%3Ar%2C%7B%221%22%3A%22RI%3A9%22%7D.

9. Helen Pidd, "Indian Blackout Held No Fear for Small Hamlet Where the Power Stayed On," *The Guardian,* September 10, 2012, http://www.theguardian.com/world/2012/sep/10/india-hamlet-where-power-stayed-on.

10. "Ashden India Renewable Energy Collective," *Ashden* (website), http://www.ashden.org/india-renewable-energy-collective.

11. "Electricity Sector in India," *Wikipedia,* http://en.wikipedia.org/wiki/Electricity_sector_in_India.

12. http://www.who.int/features/2014/clean-household-energy/en/; http://www.sciencemag.org/content/334/6053/180.full#xref-ref-10-1; http://solarcooking.wikia.com/wiki/Household_air_pollution; http://www-wds.worldbank.org/external/default/WDSContentServer/WDSP/IB/2004/05/18/000090341_20040518133631/Rendered/PDF/284380Indoor0air0no.07.pdf.

13. Ibid.

14. "List of Islands of Indonesia," *Wikipedia,* http://en.wikipedia.org/wiki/List_of_islands_of_Indonesia.

15. "Indonesia and Energy," The World Bank, http://web.worldbank.org/WBSITE/EXTERNAL/COUNTRIES/EASTASIAPACIFICEXT/EXTEAPREGTOPENERGY/0,contentMDK:20506301~pagePK:34004173~piPK:34003707~theSitePK:574015,00.html.

16. Makhtar Diop, "Powering Up Africa's Renewable Energy Revolution," Nasikiliza (blog), The World Bank, http://blogs.worldbank.org/nasikiliza/powering-africa-s-renewable-energy-revolution.

17. "African Energy Summary" (maps), GENI (Global Energy Network Institute), http://www.geni.org/globalenergy/library/national_energy_grid/africa/africanelectricitygrid.shtm.

18. Matt Rosenberg, "Largest Continent—The World's Largest Continent," About.com, About Education, http://geography.about.com/od/lists/a/large continent.htm; Diop, "Powering Up Africa's Renewable Energy Revolution."
19. "Fact Sheet: The World Bank and Energy in Africa," The World Bank, http://web.worldbank.org/WBSITE/EXTERNAL/COUNTRIES/AFR ICAEXT/0,contentMDK:21935594~pagePK:146736~piPK:146830~theSi tePK:258644,00.html.
20. Diop, "Powering Up Africa's Renewable Energy Revolution."
21. "How Many Countries Are in Africa?" Infoplease, http://www.infoplease .com/askeds/countries-africa.html.
22. "Electric Power Consumption (kWh Per Capita)," The World Bank, http:// data.worldbank.org/indicator/EG.USE.ELEC.KH.PC.
23. "Universal Access to Energy Would Herald Enormous Economic and Social Benefits," International Energy Agency, June 14, 2012, http://www.iea.org /newsroomandevents/news/2012/june/universal-access-to-energy-would -herald-enormous-economic-and-social-benefits.html.
24. "World Energy Outlook: Access to Electricity," International Energy Agency, http://www.worldenergyoutlook.org/resources/energydevelopment/access toelectricity.
25. "Universal Access to Energy Would Herald Enormous Economic and So- cial Benefits," International Energy Agency, http://www.iea.org/newsroom andevents/news/2012/june/universal-access-to-energy-would-herald-enor mous-economic-and-social-benefits.html.
26. "Coal in South Africa," *Wikipedia*, http://en.wikipedia.org/wiki/Coal_in _South_Africa.
27. Solar Energy East Africa (website), http://africa.solarenergyevents.com; "Fact Sheet: The World Bank and Energy in Africa," The World Bank; Makhtar Diop, "Powering Up Africa's Renewable Energy Revolution."
28. "World Energy Outlook: Access to Electricity," International Energy Agency.
29. "Energy Integration in Central America: Full Steam Ahead," IDB, Inter- American Development Bank, June 25, 2013, http://www.iadb.org/en/news /webstories/2013-06-25/energy-integration-in-central-america,10494.html.
30. "Energy in Latin America and the Caribbean," IDB, Inter-American De- velopment Bank, http://www.iadb.org/en/topics/energy/energy-in-latin-am erica-and-the-caribbean,1272.html; Rigoberto Ariel Yepez-García, Todd M. Johnson, and Luis Alberto Andrés, "Meeting the Electricity Supply/ Demand Balance in Latin America & the Caribbean," The World Bank, September 2010. https://esmap.org/sites/esmap.org/files/REPORT%20 LAC%20Electricity%20Challenge%20octubre%202010%20LES MAP%20FINAL.pdf; "Frequently Asked Questions about Antarctica," Cool Antarctica, http://www.coolantarctica.com/Antarctica%20fact%20 file/frequently_asked_questions.htm.
31. "When Measuring Energy Poverty, the Best and Latest Data Come from the IEA," International Energy Agency, March 7, 2014, http://www.iea .org/newsroomandevents/news/2014/march/whenmeasuringenergypoverty thebestandlatestdatacomefromtheiea.html.

CHAPTER 6: THE DARK SIDE OF POWER

1. "About Planet Solar Inc," Renewable Energy World.Com, http://www.re newableenergyworld.com/rea/companies/planet-solar-inc/about.
2. Ken Silverstein, "India and U.S. Share Energy Woes: Stealing Electricity," *Forbes,* August 5, 2012, http://www.forbes.com/sites/kensilverstein/2012/08 /05/india-and-u-s-share-energy-woes-stealing-electricity.
3. Ibid.
4. "28 Elephants Electrocuted in the Last Two Years," *The Hindu,* http://www .thehindu.com/news/national/karnataka/28-elephants-electrocuted-in-the -last-two-years/article3353679.ece.
5. "Electricity Production from Coal Sources (% of Total) in India," *Trading Economics,* http://www.tradingeconomics.com/india/electricity-production -from-coal-sources-percent-of-total-wb-data.html. also http://www.china faqs.org/issue/coal-electricity.
6. "Proposed Coal-Fired Plants Installed by Capacity (MW)," World Resources Institute, http://www.wri.org/resources/data-visualizations/propo sed-coal-fired-plants-installed-capacity-mw.
7. "Longest Trains," *Wikipedia,* http://en.wikipedia.org/wiki/Longest_trains.
8. "How Coal Works," Union of Concerned Scientists, http://www.ucsusa.org /clean_energy/coalvswind/brief_coal.html#.VWyPQlEmlDQ.
9. Ibid.
10. Peter Fairley, "A Coal Plant That Buries Its Greenhouse Gases," *MIT Technology Review,* http://www.technologyreview.com/demo/533351/a-coal -plant-that-buries-its-greenhouse-gases/?utm_campaign=newsletters&utm _source=newsletter-daily-all&utm_medium=email&utm_content=2014 1211.
11. Bryan Walsh, "Bye-Bye, Carbon: The U.S. Is (Slowly) Winning the Emissions War," *Time,* October 22, 2013, http://nation.time.com/2013/10/22 /efficiency-natural-gas-keep-pushing-u-s-carbon-emissions-down.
12. "About Planet Solar Inc," Renewable Energy World.Com, http://www.re newableenergyworld.com/rea/companies/planet-solar-inc/about.
13. "Animation of Hydraulic Fracturing (Fracking)," film by Marathon Oil Corp., https://www.youtube.com/watch?v=VY34PQUiwOQ.
14. "Fracking Explained: Opportunity or Danger?" film by Kurz Gesagt/In a Nutshell, https://www.youtube.com/watch?v=Uti2niW2BRA; Jad Mouawad and Clifford Krauss, "Dark Side of Natural Gas Boom," *New York Times,* December 7, 2009, http://www.nytimes.com/2009/12/08/business/energy -environment/08fracking.html?pagewanted=all&_r=0.
15. Ibid.
16. Nick Ramsey, "New Study Links Oklahoma Earthquakes to Fracking," MS NBC, July 8, 2014, http://www.msnbc.com/the-last-word/oklahoma-earth quakes-linked-fracking-study.
17. Ibid.
18. Oklahoma Geological Survey, http://earthquakes.ok.gov/what-we-are-doing /oklahoma-geological-survey/.

19. M. D. Petersen, C. S. Mueller, M. P. Moschetti, S. M. Hoover, J. L. Rubinstein, A. L. Llenos, A. J. Michael, W. L. Ellsworth, A. F. McGarr, A. A. Holland, and J. G. Anderson, 2015, "Incorporating Induced Seismicity in the 2014 United States National Seismic Hazard Model—Results of 2014 Workshop and Sensitivity Studies," U.S. Geological Survey Open-File Report 2015–1070, p. 69, http://dx.doi.org/10.3133/ofr20151070.

20. Andrew Childers, "EPA Underestimates Fracking's Impact on Climate Change," The Grid, *Bloomberg Business*, May 9, 2014, http://www.bloomberg.com/news/2014-05-09/epa-underestimates-fracking-s-impact-on-climate-change.html; Union of Concerned Scientists, position paper, "UCS Position on Natural Gas Extraction and Use for Electricity and Transportation in the United States," http://www.ucsusa.org/sites/default/files/legacy/assets/documents/clean_energy/UCS-Position-on-Natural-Gas-Extraction-and-Use-for-Electricity-and-Transportation-in-the-United-States.pdf.

21. "Rhodium Group Report on Global Oil & Gas Methane Emissions," Environmental Defense Fund, http://www.edf.org/climate/rhodium-group-report-global-oil-gas-methane-emissions?_ga=1.219423705.1787517823.1427851088.

22. "Chernobyl Accident," February 2, 1977, film of original Russian broadcast, https://www.youtube.com/watch?v=sC7n_QgJRks.

23. Steven Starr, "Costs and Consequences of the Fukushima Daiichi Disaster," Physicians for Social Responsibility (website), http://www.psr.org/environment-and-health/environmental-health-policy-institute/responses/costs-and-consequences-of-fukushima.html.

24. "Nuclear Energy," United States Environmental Protection Agency (website), http://epa.gov/cleanenergy/energy-and-you/affect/nuclear.html.

CHAPTER 7: THE FUTURE OF POWER

1. "Batteries Included? The Search for Better Ways of Storing Electricity is Hotting Up," *The Economist*, February 2, 2013, http://www.economist.com/news/science-and-technology/21571117-search-better-ways-storing-electricity-hotting-up-batteries.

2. Sarah Griffiths, "The World's First Island Powered Entirely by Wind and a Lake That's a Huge Battery: Spain's El Hierro Will Take Advantage of Gusts from African Coast," *Daily Mail*, April 28, 2014, http://www.dailymail.co.uk/sciencetech/article-2614804/Spanish-island-world-powered-entirely-wind-water.html; http://www.outsideonline.com/news-from-the-field/El-Hierro-First-Energy-Self-Sufficient-Island.html.

3. "Batteries Included? The Search for Better Ways of Storing Electricity," *The Economist*.

4. "Duke Energy Renewables Completes Notrees Battery Storage Project in Texas; North America's Largest Battery Storage Project at a Wind Farm," Duke Energy (website), January 23, 2013, http://www.duke-energy.com/news/releases/2013012301.asp.

5. "Notrees, Texas," *Wikipedia*, https://en.wikipedia.org/wiki/Notrees%2C_Texas.

6. "Duke Energy Renewables Completes Notrees Battery Storage Project."
7. Nouber Afeyan, "Top 10 Emerging Technologies for 2014" World Economic Forum, Agenda, September 1, 2014, https://forumblog.org/2014/09/top-ten-emerging-technologies-2014/#electricity-storage.
8. Kevin Bullis, "A Promising Step Toward Round-the-Clock Solar Power," *MIT Technology Review,* September 26, 2014, http://www.technologyreview.com/news/531141/a-promising-step-toward-round-the-clock-solar-power/.
9. "Plug Power Receives Milestone Order from Walmart for Multi-Site Hydrogen Fuel Cell Deployment," Plug Power (website), February 26, 2014, http://www.plugpower.com/news/pressreleases/14-02-26/PLUG_POWER_RECEIVES_MILESTONE_ORDER_FROM_WALMART_FOR_MULTI-SITE_HYDROGEN_FUEL_CELL_DEPLOYMENT.aspx.
10. "BAT: The Buoyant Airborne Turbine," Altaeros Energies (website), http://www.altaerosenergies.com/bat.html.
11. Megan Garber, "The Windmill of the Future Could Be Floating in the Sky," *The Atlantic,* March 27, 2014, http://www.theatlantic.com/technology/archive/2014/03/the-windmill-of-the-future-could-be-floating-in-the-sky/359706/; Chris Nelder, "Are Methane Hydrates Really Going to Change Geopolitics?" *The Atlantic,* May 2, 2013, http://www.theatlantic.com/technology/archive/2013/05/are-methane-hydrates-really-going-to-change-geopolitics/275275/?single_page=true.
12. Charles C. Mann, "What If We Never Run Out of Oil?" *The Atlantic,* April 24, 2014, http://www.theatlantic.com/magazine/archive/2013/05/what-if-we-never-run-out-of-oil/309294/.
13. Gareth Cook, "A New Way to Do Nuclear," *The New Yorker,* June 13, 2013, http://www.newyorker.com/tech/elements/a-new-way-to-do-nuclear.
14. https://www.solveforx.com/moonshot/5648554290839552.
15. "Power from Nuclear Waste," film by Leslie Dewan, Solve for X, https://www.youtube.com/watch?v=4UXXwWOImm8.
16. "Creating a Safe, Secure, Energy Source," TerraPower (website), http://terrapower.com/pages/technology.
17. Cook, "A New Way to Do Nuclear."
18. Brian Handwerk, "Five Striking Concepts for Harnessing the Sea's Power," *National Geographic,* February 21, 2014, http://news.nationalgeographic.com/news/energy/2014/02/140220-five-striking-wave-and-tidal-energy-concepts/.
19. "The Power of Smart Design," Aquamarine Power (website), http://www.aquamarinepower.com; "Investor Relations Overview," Ocean Power Technologies (website), http://phx.corporate-ir.net/phoenix.zhtml?c=155437&p=irol-IRHome.

CHAPTER 8: THE COMING MICROGRIDS

1. Allison Lantero, "How Microgrids Work," Energy.Gov, June 17, 2014, http://energy.gov/articles/how-microgrids-work.

2. "Microgrids for Rural Electrification: A Critical Review of Best Practices Based on Seven Case Studies," United Nations Foundation with Carnegie Mellon University and the University of California at Berkeley, February 2014.

3. "Rural Energy Alternatives in India," Woodrow Wilson School at Princeton University, February 2014.

4. "Microgrids for Rural Electrification: A Critical Review of Best Practices Based on Seven Case Studies," United Nations Foundation with Carnegie Mellon University and the University of California at Berkeley, February 2014.

5. "Powerhive Inc.: First Solar Backed Off-Grid Innovator to Capitalize on Kenya Experience,". *Marketwatch,* 4/28/2015, press release http://www .marketwatch.com/story/powerhive-inc-first-solar-backed-off-grid-innova tor-to-capitalize-on-kenya-experience-2015-04-28.

6. Kevin Bullis, "A Billion People in the Dark," *MIT Technology Review,* October 24, 2012.

7. "Remote Microgrids Will Surpass $8.4 Billion in Annual Revenue by 2020," *Navigant Research,* September 25, 2013, http://www.navigantre search.com/newsroom/remote-microgrids-will-surpass-8-4-billion-in-an nual-revenue-by-2020.

8. Laurie Guevara-Stone, "How Microgrids Can Help Developing Nations Leapfrog the Landline," GreenBiz, August 1, 2013, http://www .greenbiz.com/blog/2013/08/01/how-microgrids-can-help-developing-na tions-leapfrog-landline.

9. Lisa Cohn, "Obama Visit Could Help Boost India's Microgrid Market," *Microgrid Knowledge,* January 28, 2015, http://microgridknowledge.com /obama-visit-help-boost-indias-microgrid-market/.

10. "SharedSolar: Lighting Up Rural Africa," a film by SharedSolar, January 9, 2013, https://www.youtube.com/watch?x-yt-ts=1422579428&x-yt-cl=8511 4404&v=8IPM2oH8IAo#t=181.

11. Sebastian Groh, Daniel Philipp, Brian Edlefsen Lasch, Hannes Kirchhoff, "Swarm Electrification—Suggesting a Paradigm Change through Building Microgrids Bottom-Up," paper, accessed via http://ieeexplore.ieee.org/xpl /articleDetails.jsp?arnumber=6861710&punumber%3D6853542%26sortT ype%3Dasc_p_Sequence%26filter%3DAND(p_IS_Number%3A6861645) %26pageNumber%3D3.

CHAPTER 9: ATTRACTING CAPITAL

1. Global BrightLight Foundation Internal presentation document by Jake Reeder, MPP/MBA candidate, Duke University, 2015.

2. Global BrightLight Foundation, internal presentation by Jake Reader, MPP/ MBA candidate, Duke University, 2015.

3. http://www.fastcompany.com/1749253/fighting-water-borne-disease-africa -and-making-millions-process; http://www.bloomberg.com/news/articles /2012-03-09/gold-standard-wins-voluntary-co2-credits-for-kenya-water -filters.

4. Katherine Deaton Steel, "Energy System Development in Africa: The Case of Grid and Off-Grid Power in Kenya," Ph.D. dissertation, MIT, 2008.
5. Vera Von Kreutzbruck, "India: Solar Cheaper than Grid Power," *PV Magazine*, April 4, 2013, http://www.pv-magazine.com/news/details/beitrag/india-solar-cheaper-than-grid-power_100010792/#axzz2ZzVu648w.
6. "Solar Lighting—Lighting the Way," *The Economist*, September 1, 2012, http://www.economist.com/node/21560983.

CHAPTER 10: OVERCOMING BARRIERS
ON THE ROAD AHEAD

1. Jake Kendall and Roger Voorhies, "The Mobile-Finance Revolution," *Foreign Affairs*, March/April 2014, http://www.foreignaffairs.com/articles/140733/jake-kendall-and-rodger-voorhies/the-mobile-finance-revolution.
2. Ibid.
3. Rachel Kleinfeld and Drew Sloan, *Let There Be Light: Electrifying the Developing World with Markets and Distributed Energy* (Washington, D.C.: Truman National Security Project, 2012), pp. 84–91.

INDEX